# Clinical Counselling in Context

Professional counselling practice is full of complexities and subtleties, yet the richness of clinical counselling still receives insufficient recognition in the literature and in public opinion. In the light of the current professionalization of counselling, *Clinical Counselling in Context: An Introduction* examines the hypothesis that counselling theory and practice are altered by the specific organisational context in which it takes place. Looking at various types of therapeutic work, its central idea is that there is a complex inter-relationship between clinical work and context, and that working with the dynamics of the context can be an important force for therapeutic change.

The opening chapters of the book explore the broader spectrum of ideas and assumptions that underpin clinical counselling, covering such themes as postmodernism, research, clinical practice, pragmatism and managed care. Subsequent chapters examine the engagement between the clinician and the setting in which s/he works from a number of perspectives. Final chapters return to the broader perspective, this time emphasizing the interaction between the consulting room and society at large.

Theoretical and clinical sophistication is often associated with psychotherapeutic practice, while counselling is seen as a simpler and more superficial activity. *Clinical Counselling in Context: An Introduction* challenges this assumption. It argues that, with sufficient professionalization and a well-thought-out academic base, counselling can be a sophisticated activity which is not just the poor neighbour of psychotherapy.

**John Lees** is Senior Lecturer in Counselling and runs the post-graduate training course in counselling at the University of Greenwich. He is a UKRC registered independent counsellor and works as a counsellor and supervisor in a variety of settings. He is a member of the British Association for Psychoanalytic and Psychodynamic Supervision and is also editor of the journal *Psychodynamic Counselling*.

Contributors: Pat Grant; Adrian Hemmings; Gordon Lynch; June Roberts; Andrew Samuels; Michael Scott; Alison Vaspe; Kitty Warburton.

**Clinical Counselling in Context**
Series editor: John Lees

This series of key texts examines the unique nature of counselling in a wide range of clinical settings. Each book shows how the context in which counselling takes place has profound effects on the nature and outcome of the counselling practice, and encourages clinical debate and dialogue.

**Clinical Counselling in Context**
An Introduction
*Edited by John Lees*

**Clinical Counselling in Primary Care**
*Edited by John Lees*

**Clinical Counselling in Further and Higher Education**
*Edited by John Lees and Alison Vaspe*

# Clinical Counselling in Context
## An Introduction

**Edited by John Lees**

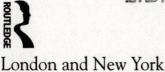

London and New York

First published 1999 by Routledge
11 New Fetter Lane, London EC4P 4EE

Simultaneously published in the USA and Canada
by Routledge
29 West 35th Street, New York, NY 10001

Typeset in Goudy by Keystroke, Jacaranda Lodge, Wolverhampton
Printed and bound in Great Britain by Clays Ltd, St Ives PLC

*British Library Cataloguing in Publication Data*
A catalogue record for this book is available from the British Library

*Library of Congress Cataloging in Publication Data*
Clinical counselling in context : an introduction /
    edited by John Lees.
        p.     cm. — (Clinical counselling in context
series)
    Includes bibliographical references and index.
    1. Mental health counseling.   2. Clinical
psychology.   I. Lees, John, 1951–  .  II. Series.
    [DNLM: 1. Counseling.  2. Psychotherapy—methods.
3. Psychology, Clinical.  WM 55 C6407 1999]
RC466.C55   1999
362.2'04256—dc21
DNLM/DLC
for Library of Congress                                          98–29006
                                                                     CIP

ISBN 0–415–17955–6 (hbk)
ISBN 0–415–17956–4 (pbk)

# Contents

# Figures and table

## Figures

## Table

# Contributors

**Pat Grant** MSc, BEd (Hons), DN, RGN, RMN, SCM is a registered independent counsellor and a BAC accredited supervisor. She works at the University of Greenwich where she is engaged in teacher preparation for higher and further education lectures. Pat is also involved in the training and education of counsellors. Her main areas of interest within the field of counselling are bereavement and issues related to race and culture.

**Adrian Hemmings** D.Phil. has worked as a Research Fellow at the University of Sussex for nearly ten years. His research interests are in psychological interventions in GP practices. Before then he worked for several years as a group therapist in a therapeutic community. He continues to run and evaluate groups for patients in primary care, particularly with those who somatise. He has a small private practice.

**John Lees** is Senior Lecturer in Counselling and Pathway Leader in postgraduate counselling training at the University of Greenwich. He is a UKRC registered independent counsellor and a member of the British Association for Psychoanalytic and Psychodynamic Supervision. He works as a counsellor and supervisor in private practice, community counselling and primary care, is author of numerous articles on counselling and editor of *Psychodynamic Counselling*.

**Gordon Lynch** PhD is Lecturer in Counselling at University College Chester. His academic backround is in theology and he maintains an interest in the role of theological and philosophical reflection for understanding counselling. His current interests also include the significance of postmodernism and narrative theories for counselling as well as the application of Kohut's self psychology to counselling practice. The majority of his counselling work has been with young people in the context of the voluntary sector.

**June Roberts** began her working life in Fry's chocolate factory and as a houseparent in 'approved schools' for young offenders. She then joined Family Service Units, working in Liverpool and East London. Her social work qualifications were obtained at Bristol University and later in the Department of Sociology at Surrey University. She is a life-member of the Institute of Psychotherapy and Social Studies, and Co-ordinator of Time-Limited Counselling at the Westminster Pastoral Foundation. She teaches brief psychotherapy and social issues at Regent's College School of Psychotherapy and Counselling, where she enjoys a healthy exposure to the values and methods of existential phenomenology.

**Andrew Samuels** is Professor of Analytical Psychology at the University of Essex and a Jungian training analyst. He is a scientific associate of the American Academy of Psychoanalysis and a member of the Association for Humanistic Psychology. He is a founder-member of Psychotherapists and Counsellors for Social Responsibility and of Antidote, a psychotherapy- based think-tank. His books, which have been translated into some eighteen languages, include *Jung and the Post-Jungians* (1985), *A Critical Dictionary of Jungian Analysis* (1986), *The Father* (1986), *The Plural Psyche* (1989), *Psychopathology* (1989), *The Political Psyche* (1993), and *The Secret Life of Politics* (forthcoming 2000).

**Michael Scott** PhD is a chartered counselling psychologist and Honorary Research Fellow in the Department of Psychology at the University of Manchester. He is the author of five books, a number of book chapters and numerous papers. He is also consultant psychologist to ICI, Merseyside Police, Glaxo and Littlewoods and works one and a half days a week in the NHS.

**Alison Vaspe** studied music and worked in publishing before training as a counsellor at Westminster Pastoral Foundation and Birkbeck College, London University. She then completed the Guild of Psychotherapists/ University of Hertfordshire MA in psychoanalytic psychotherapy, for which her research subject was counselling women medical students. She works as a counsellor at King's College, London and at the Marylebone Health Centre, and is the co-author with Marilyn Miller-Pietroni of *Inside Counselling in Primary Care*. She is also associate editor of the journal *Psychodynamic Counselling*.

**Kitty Warburton** is a UKCP registered integrative psychotherapist who currently works as a counsellor for De Montfort University. Prior to training in counselling and psychotherapy at Regent's College, London she trained as a teacher and has taught in the secondary, further, higher and adult education sectors. She has a special interest in boundary issues and time-limited work.

# Acknowledgements

Several people have provided help and encouragement in the process of assembling this volume. In particular, however, I would like to thank all those people who helped to peer review the chapters, as well as the forbearance of the contributors in doing what was needed to be done and in meeting deadlines (more or less). Finally, I wish to thank Ellen Noonan and the staff of the counselling trainings at Birkbeck College who first planted the idea of the contextual nature of counselling in my mind.

Most of the contributions to this volume appear for the first time, with the exception of chapter 6, 'Establishing a therapeutic frame', by Kitty Warburton, which is a modified version of a paper which appeared in 1995 as 'Student counselling: a consideration of ethical and framework issues' in *Psychodynamic Counselling* 1(3): 421–437.

# Introduction

*John Lees*

This book takes the view that the development of the talking cure has taken a radical new change in direction since the 1970s and that this is linked with the development of counselling as a distinct activity within the broad field of psychological therapy. Counselling can be distinguished from other forms of talking therapy (such as psychotherapy and psycho-analysis) in several ways – it is accessible to greater numbers of people, it tends to take place in a variety of organizational contexts and, because of its organizational and contextual nature, counsellors are exposed to a whole range of social, political and organizational issues and may, in different ways, take these into account in their work. Furthermore, it often involves working with practitioners from different theoretical persuasions. Looking at this from a broader conceptual perspective, this book will present the view that counselling is a quintessentially postmodern activity. For example, it will take the view that its differentiated contextual nature lends itself to a flexible approach to the application of theory to practice. Indeed one could say that the most appropriate clinical practice at any one time is the one that best fits that particular situation. This corresponds with Lyotard's (1992) view that universally applied theories, or 'metanarratives', are redundant. It thus differs from the viewpoint that says that there are right and wrong ways of conducting our clinical practice. This perhaps explains why there are so many different versions of talking therapy today. Indeed, it sometimes seems as though there are as many variants as there are practitioners.

In view of these principles, the book aims to create a space where different viewpoints about clinical counselling in context can be expressed. However, it is clearly impossible to do full justice to the many variants of counselling, so the emphasis will be on providing a glimpse of the range of applications and ideas in the field. In so doing the book does not have a polemical intent. It is not meant to show the superiority of one view over another. Instead it will adopt a phenomenological approach – it will put different viewpoints side by side and attempt to show how they create a variety and richness which can then produce something new. Indeed, this approach has been influenced by the principle of the Socratic dialogue, which was applied by Hegel to the evolution of ideas, by Marx to economic, social and political development, by Goethe to scientific thinking (Uberoi 1984), by Samuels (1993) to training, and by Jung to his understanding of the human psyche with his emphasis on the complementariness of opposites – anima and animus, yin and yang. As Jung (cited in Gordon 1993: 7) says: 'if a union is to take place between opposites like Spirit and Matter, Conscious and Unconscious, bright and dark and so on, it will happen in a third thing, which represents not a compromise but something new'. In this book the same principle has been applied to the different viewpoints on clinical practice. It is a viewpoint, moreover, which I have called 'clinical counselling in context'.

The notions of differentiation and polarity form two threads which interweave through the book. Overall it can be divided into three parts. The first part (chapters 1 to 3) looks at counselling in context from the point of view of meta-theory. In different ways these chapters examine the broader spectrum of ideas and assumptions that underpin clinical counselling. They cover a range of overlapping themes such as postmodernism, research, clinical practice, pragmatism and managed care. They illustrate the differentiated nature of counselling and some of the tensions, or polarities, in the profession. The second part (chapters 4 to 7) looks specifically at clinical work. Adopting different clinical perspectives, the authors of these chapters examine the engagement between the clinician and the setting in which s/he is working, between the consulting room and the broader context. Pure theory becomes transformed as it is applied in different contexts. The chapters can also be read as a dialogue between the different viewpoints expressed by the authors, inasmuch as they present different perspectives on similar clinical issues. Finally, chapters 8 and 9 return to the broader perspective. This time, however, the emphasis is on the interaction, or 'dialogue', between the consulting room and society at large, between clinical work and society, culture and politics.

The first three chapters look at some underlying polarities in our profession. In 'What is clinical counselling in context? (chapter 1) John Lees examines the way in which we see counselling today. He surveys a range of viewpoints on both clinical practice and research. Then he looks at various attempts that have been made to define it, and tries to show how definitions will always be limited, subjective and ephemeral. In so doing he examines such polarities as objective and subjective, product and process. Gordon Lynch, in chapter 2, entitled, 'A pragmatic approach to clinical counselling in context', examines the tension between positivism and pragmatism in the counselling profession, between the assumption that 'if a therapeutic theory is true then it can be applied to client work regardless of when, where or with whom the therapy takes place' and one which 'holds that each specific situation is different', between an approach to counselling based on the perceived truthfulness of a theoretical position and its usefulness as a therapy. Finally, in chapter 3, entitled 'Assessment of psychological change and the future practice of clinical counselling', Adrian Hemmings examines the polarity between clinical practice and counselling research. How important for clinicians are the questions usually asked by researchers? Is it helpful to ask whether it works, how it works, and how its efficiency can be improved? Is the notion of managed care a step forward for clinical counselling or is it a notion that de-humanizes therapeutic practice?

The second part of the book concentrates on clinical practice. The chapters are written from different theoretical and clinical perspectives and are intended to show how different clinical viewpoints can complement each other: how they create a professional field of activity which is alive and mutually fructifying rather than remote, cut off, incestuous and arid. Chapters 4 and 5 both look at short-term work from differing perspectives. In 'Time-limited work in context' June Roberts contrasts time-limited psychodynamic work with long-term work. She discusses the merits of both and shows that time-limited work has an important part to play in thera-peutic practice. She does so from the perspective of a psychodynamic psychotherapist – a viewpoint which has traditionally seen therapeutic practice in terms of long-term developmental work. In 'The problem-solving pilgrim: a goal-orientated approach to clinical counselling', on the other hand, Michael Scott takes a different view of short-term work. He approaches it from a problem-solving, cognitive-behavioural perspective and, as such, this contains no assumptions about the desirability of long-term vis-à-vis short-term work. By a process of clarifying the problem so that it is solvable, applying specific therapeutic techniques and evaluating progress, the emphasis is on achieving optimum results in the shortest possible time. Chapters 6 and 7 both examine the therapeutic framework and the therapeutic space from different points of view. In 'Establishing a therapeutic frame' Kitty Warburton argues the case for establishing and maintaining boundaries when we are working in environments that make it difficult to do so – people bursting in on sessions, appointments being made by receptionists, and so on. She argues that these break the frame and disrupt the therapeutic possibilities of the work. In contrast Alison Vaspe, in 'The therapeutic space and relationship', sees the interactions taking place in the space contained by the framework as being the crucial factor in therapeutic work. She examines the subtleties of the client–counsellor interaction which take place within this space and shows how they are influenced by the overall context of the work. Utilizing Winnicott's notion of 'potential space' she sees this interaction as 'an arena in which a particular kind of emotional experience can take place'.

The two final chapters look at the interaction between clinical work and the broader cultural, social and political context. In 'Issues of cultural difference in staff teams and client work' Pat Grant examines the importance of informing ourselves about the cultural background of our colleagues and clients. She also looks at the important issue of identity development: how it can influence the way people from different cultures respond to us, and how the failure of practitioners to understand identity development can lead to misunderstanding. Finally, Andrew Samuels, in 'Working directly with political, social and cultural material in the therapy session', examines the link between the consulting room and politics. He looks at the tension between the personal/intrapsychic and the external/political. Instead of discussing how clinical practice is influenced by context he presents the relatively unfamiliar viewpoint that the personal can also be political, that the intrapsychic can be the basis for engaging with the world.

The viewpoints represented in this book clearly reflect different theoretical approaches, assumptions and beliefs regarding clinical practice and counselling research. They range from those concerned with achieving results which can be quantified, to those concerned with developing technique and theoretical understanding. Furthermore, the viewpoints about technique range from those that see it as a pure activity, to those that see it as an applied activity which is changed by the context in which it takes place. Yet they all have something useful to say. Human experience is so complex that different theoretical and clinical perspectives are inevitable.

In conclusion, it is worth reminding ourselves that our profession, because of its differentiated nature, is still prone to conflict, schism and dispute. The principle of polarity can create a malign as well as a benign outcome. There is a temptation to dismiss and disparage people who hold standpoints that are different from one's own. An example of this is the dispute about professionalization, regulation, accreditation, and registration. There are those who believe this is a good thing: the principal professional bodies in the field, for instance – the British Association for Counselling, the United Kingdom Council of Psychotherapy, the British Confederation of Psychotherapists, and the British Psychological Society. Yet there are others who take the view that regulation would be a 'disaster' (House & Totton 1997: 1). Clearly the profession is divided into two camps. Such debates, moreover, are usually conducted on the basis that one viewpoint is correct and the other incorrect, with a resulting tendency towards fragmentation and suspicion. However, there is a third possibility – namely that both viewpoints are necessary and important. Without professionalization, counselling and psychotherapy would continue to be viewed as dilettante activities that can be practised by anyone who has done a weekend course in counselling, thereby providing the opportunity for negative column space in the newspapers. On the other hand, without the anti-professionalization viewpoint, the profession may become over-regulated, too elitist, and subsumed by power struggles, to the detriment of our clients. Perhaps a creative tension between these two extremes is the most healthy scenario. Such a 'middle way' is, by and large, the position adopted by this book with regard to differing views about the fundamental nature of counselling, clinical practice, social, cultural and political life, as well as profession-wide disputes.

## References

Gordon, R. (1993), *Bridges*, London: Karnac Books.

House, R. and Totton, N. (1997), *Implausible Professions: Arguments for Pluralism and Autonomy in Psychotherapy and Counselling*, Ross-on-Wye, UK: PCCS Books.

Lyotard, J.-F. (1992), *The Postmodern Condition: A Report on Knowledge*, Manchester: Manchester University Press.

Samuels, A. (1993), 'What is a good training?', *British Journal of Psychotherapy*, 9(3): 317–324.

Uberoi, J.P.S. (1984), *The Other Mind of Europe: Goethe as Scientist*, Delhi: Oxford University Press.

# 1   What is clinical counselling in context?

*John Lees*

Plans fail for lack of counsel,
but with many advisers they succeed.
(Proverbs, 15:22)

This chapter will look at different perspectives on the talking cure over the last hundred years, from the point of both view of clinical practice and academic research. It will then identify some of the underlying trends in the profession and look at counselling as a specific development within the history of psychological therapy as a whole. These considerations, more-over, will form the foundation of the chapter, which will conclude by defining clinical counselling in context and showing how it is applied in practice. Overall, I believe that this undertaking is part of a much broader process that is currently taking place, which I would describe as coun-selling's 'coming of age' – a process which, in view of the rapid growth of counselling in recent years, involves asking such questions as: what is the place of counselling in the profession as a whole? How can it be dis-tinguished from other talking therapies such as psychotherapy? Does it have a distinct identity?

## The evolution of talking therapy

For thousands of years there has been a tradition of talking therapy (see, for instance, Ellenberger 1970). However, I would date the systematic development of the talking therapy in modern post-Enlightenment times from the work of Breuer and Freud at the end of the nineteenth century, so this is where I will begin. Significant turning points in this respect were Breuer's work with Anna O, between 1880 and 1882; Freud's earlier case studies, such as that of Elizabeth von R in 1892; Freud's first use of the term 'psychoanalysis' to describe his theories in 1896; and the publication of

Freud's *The Interpretation of Dreams* in 1900 and *Three Essays on Sexuality* in 1902. I will argue that the theories of Freud have played a central role in the development of the different talking cures until the middle of the century, affecting both the development of theory and counselling research. I will briefly examine the theoretical consequences in this section and the research consequences in the next section.

As regards theory, most of the pioneers of the talking cure encountered psychoanalysis in one form or another. You either embraced it or rejected it, but you couldn't avoid it. As W.H. Auden noted of Freud, in a poem which he wrote on Freud's death in 1939, he was 'no more a person . . . but a whole climate of opinion'. Indeed, many of the different therapies which developed in the course of this century arose – in part – as a reaction to psychoanalysis. This began with the early schismatics such as Jung and Adler, but has also included a continual stream of practitioners who were at one time involved with psychoanalysis, but went on to form their own schools of thought – such people as Fritz Perls, Carl Rogers, Aaron Beck and Albert Ellis, who were instrumental in founding the Gestalt, Person-centred and Cognitive Schools of therapy, respectively. Having said this, I fully recognize that all these practitioners were influenced by a variety of other philosophical, religious and psychological ideas: existentialism, phenomenology, religion, gestalt psychology, behavioural psychology, cognitive psychology, and so on. Yet I believe that an important strand of their thinking was that they saw psychoanalysis as limited, even mistaken. Jung, for instance, whilst still developing his friendship with Freud, had reservations about Freud's commitment to his psychosexual theory (Stevens 1990: 20), whilst cognitive therapists such as Beck and Ellis saw the whole notion of the unconscious (and psychoanalytic perspectives on early childhood development) as unscientific, and psychoanalytic therapeutic technique, such as interpretation, as subjective and speculative.

In view of these differences – the breakaway movements, the development of distinct therapies, and so on – the overall picture is thus of an ever-increasing network of therapies, with new branches being created all the time. For the purposes of this discussion, I will just point out four features of this development. First, it has led to a tremendous variety of outlooks which make up the profession (numbering some 450 according to Corsini, cited in Clarkson 1996: 143). Second, the profession has been subjected to an ever greater process of fragmentation. Not only did people form distinct schools, but within many schools there has been a splintering process: schools within schools. The Freudians split into the Freudians, the 'Middle Group' and the Kleinians, whilst the Jungians split into the Archetypal School and the Developmental School, the Person-centred

School split into the purists and the integrationists, and so on. Indeed, there are now also the integrative schools which, in effect, form a fourth school of therapy, and are again divided into different schools. Third, it has led to many practitioners becoming isolated from their contemporaries in the profession, with a resulting tendency to regard other practitioners with suspicion and strive to maintain distinctness, purity and separateness. Yet one could argue perhaps that such tendencies were natural in the so-called Age of Modernism with its emphasis on the notion of the Grand Theory. Finally, in its extreme form, this process of isolation from peers can result in polarization and conflict – even bitterness. What about the academic perspective? Can the same features be observed?

## The academic perspective

The academic perspective – particularly in psychology departments – usually consists of research into the efficacy of counselling and psychotherapy and its status as a science. Essentially the questions researchers ask are: Does it work? If so, how?

Research has not, over the years, been a primary feature of the work of most clinicians. Indeed, I think it would be fair to say that clinicians have been more interested in the development of theories and clinical techniques than research. This may have been influenced to some extent by the development of the profession. Perhaps this is a second legacy left by Freud. His research methods were confined to case studies and he essentially eschewed conventional experimental methods (Hill & Corbett 1993: 3) – a pattern that has, arguably, influenced the psychodynamic and, to some extent, the humanistic traditions ever since. Essentially, the development of psychoanalytic technique and thinking was based on a lengthy and intensive process of self-reflection, hypothesizing about clinical experience and reviewing theory and technique in the light of these reflections. It is thus essentially a subjective activity – a form of qualitative research. Many practitioners pursuing this approach would agree with the psychoanalyst Guntrip (1973) that therapy is so individualized it is difficult, if not impossible, to study it using normal experimental methods, or Arlow (1984: 24), who expresses a highly subjective view of research into therapy, stating that the psychodynamic tendency to link present difficulties with early childhood 'is not a theory; it is an empirical finding confirmed in every psychoanalysis'. In other words, the clinician's direct experience is viewed as a scientific activity. It is thus not surprising that the clinical literature abounds with case studies and that this has constituted the principal form of psychoanalytic research. This view contrasts to the commonly held pragmatic academic view that good therapy does not just depend on 'whether doctors, patients or clients like counselling or perceive it to be helpful, but whether it is effective in bringing about an improvement in symptoms or in the client's problems' (Corney 1997: 8). Indeed, some researchers are extremely critical of the subjective case study approach. The practitioner/researcher Meehl (1997: 94), for example, states, in no uncertain terms, that 'if I insist that my anecdotal impression must prevail, I am not being merely arrogant and unscholarly, I am being immoral'.

Another major form of therapy research has been process research, which can be dated from the 1930s. Hill & Corbett (1993: 4), for example, refer to recordings that were made of sessions in order to ascertain the amount of 'talk time' of therapists in counselling interviews. They then describe how more sophisticated methods of process research gradually developed, concerned with illustrating the effectiveness of counsellor interventions. They examined how counsellor interventions influenced the client's subsequent statements, and thus continued the clinician's tradition of developing new theories and clinical techniques, as opposed to evaluating outcomes and efficacy (albeit in a different manner from the psychoanalytic method). Foremost amongst these developments was the work of Carl Rogers at Ohio State University in the 1940s, which attempted to show that nondirective interventions by the therapist – such as accepting, clarifying and reflecting the feelings expressed by the client – helped clients to see themselves in a more positive light and were thus therapeutically beneficial. Indeed, this research influences the development of many basic counselling and counselling-skills trainings and, at a more advanced level, underpins some of the debates between the different theoretical orientations.

A more recent development in the research field is outcome research, which essentially dates from the 1950s. Eysenck's (1952) seminal review of the literature on psychotherapy outcomes was particularly influential. According to his analysis of the results there was a success rate of 44 per cent for psychoanalytic treatment of neurotic patients, as opposed to 64 per cent for other therapeutic approaches, and 72 per cent for two groups of comparable patients, who were not treated by any form of therapy. In other words he claimed, in effect, that therapy – and, in particular, psychoanalysis – made people worse. In saying this it should be noted that Eysenck's claims have, in turn, been challenged (for example, by Bergin 1971). He argues, for instance, that it is difficult to obtain an accurate figure for spontaneous recovery (i.e. the untreated groups) since many individuals who are denied therapy may, for example, go elsewhere and are thus not necessarily untreated. There is also the question of whether any study can be value-free. In conclusion, we are left to ponder whether Eysenck's study constitutes a scientific breakthrough or a biased attack on psychoanalysis based on distorted figures.

Whatever view we take of Eysenck, outcome research has been clearly on the agenda since his study. More recently, with the rapid expansion of counselling and the consequent need for counselling practitioners to justify the usefulness of their work to funders, it has become increasingly important. However, there is a divergence of opinion about how to evaluate outcomes, ranging from those people (such as Clarkson 1996) who favour qualitative studies using a range of subjective criteria including peer scrutiny of case studies, questionnaires, interviews and so on, to those (such as Corney 1997) who favour quantitative studies using statistical analysis and such scientific methodology as the clinical trial, which, as a result of using control groups, attempts to eliminate other possible reasons for recovery.

When we include the research, in addition to the clinical, perspective on talking therapies, the overall impression is one of yet more fragmentation, polarization and conflict. What can we make of this tremendous variety of views, often held with conviction and vehemence? How can we locate ourselves in relation to it? There are, it seems to me, two primary responses to these questions. We can take sides in the disputes and disagreements. Alternatively, we can see the different theoretical and research standpoints as all containing elements of truth. We see them, so to speak, as different perspectives rather than absolute truths. We don't just argue for a research-based objective approach based, say, on the notion of the clinical trial, or a deeper understanding of human nature based on a more subjective case study perspective, but take the view that both of these viewpoints have something to say (see Lynch 1996: 146). For instance, most clinical trials show equivocal results (Corney 1997), which is a salutory reminder to counsellors to reflect on their technique and practice for the benefit of their clients. Case studies, on the other hand, enable practitioners to portray the complexities and nuances of therapeutic work and provide a basis for reflecting on, and improving, technique and conceptual understanding.

Having surveyed 'the different' points of view in the development of the counselling profession I will now adopt an approach to these differences which will be inclusive rather than exclusive, inasmuch as it will accommodate different viewpoints on counselling. Furthermore, I feel that this is appropriate today since it fits well with the so-called postmodern age and with the complexities of the broad variety of organizational settings in which counselling is usually practised.

## The postmodern perspective

Surveying the history of the talking cure one may come to the conclusion that it is fragmented and divided, with no common standards about what constitutes good practice. This may seem, at first sight, to be a lamentable state of affairs. However, it can also be seen as a welcome diversity that is a great advantage. Indeed, this is the view held by the government and given as a reason for not imposing statutory regulation. Richardson (cited in House & Totton 1997: 2), expressing the government view, said that regulation would 'prevent that diversity and would be unwelcome' since it would exclude such therapeutic activities as stress management and some forms of psycho-educational activity. Furthermore, the diversity of perspectives is also in keeping with the prevailing postmodern *Zeitgeist*, which has been described as 'a multiplicity of fragmented, and frequently interrupted "looks"' (McRobbie 1989: 165). In other words, it is a viewpoint which says that our outlook on the complexity of existence is always limited. It is contextual rather than definitive: it provides an interpretation of existence rather than a definitive understanding (Lynch 1997: 21). Moreover, such a perspective doesn't necessarily reject the different viewpoints, but sees them as limited perspectives and part of a larger whole. It is deconstructive. It subverts the notion of the all encompassing explanation, or the Grand Theory, but accepts the place of such all encompassing theories in the pantheon of knowledge.

This postmodern view accepts that differentiation – even fragmentation and conflict – is inevitable and normal. It can be creative and needn't be destructive or divisive. It accepts the possibility of there being, on the one hand, both right and wrong viewpoints and, on the other, a multiplicity of viewpoints (Samuels: 1989). In other words, it accepts that we may sometimes take a standpoint which we believe to be right and, at other times, the apparently contrasting viewpoint. It says that thinking in terms of right and wrong is too limiting and absolutist since it leads to one-dimensional thinking in which we speak, think and converse in only one way. By accepting the validity of different viewpoints (even if we don't agree with them) we create a field of activity which is alive and creative. We engage in a dialectical process of argument and counter-argument where the different viewpoints create something entirely new rather than variations on the same theme. Indeed, it has even been argued that the mind functions in a complementary manner and that such polarities – including the possibility of conflict – are an inevitable part of healthy human development (Gordon 1993: 27).

## Postmodernism and counselling

This differentiated postmodern perspective fits very well with the circumstances of much counselling practice. Counsellors are likely to work with colleagues from many different theoretical perspectives, in a variety of different contexts where there is an awareness of social, as well as psychological, values (such as the needs of minority groups) – a fact which lends itself to holding a variety of viewpoints, and which corresponds with postmodern principles of differentiation, diversity and pluralism. Indeed, the development of counselling coincided with the emergence of post-modernism. The counselling movement generally dates from the 1970s (McLeod 1993), at least in Britain, as does the age of postmodernism (Appignanesi 1989). So although it has its roots in the development of talking therapies generally, as already described, counselling per se is a relatively recent phenomenon.

In order to both illustrate and demonstrate a differentiated postmodern approach to clinical counselling in context, I will adopt two entirely different perspectives in my attempt to define counselling. Having surveyed some of the attempts that have been made to define counselling as distinct from other talking therapies and examined my personal experience of working in different counselling milieus, I will attempt to establish a definition of clinical counselling which is both 'objective' and 'subjective'. The 'objective' definition will be based on 'a secondary form of knowledge in which we separate ourselves from that which we know' (Rose 1997: 389). The 'subjective' definition, meanwhile, will be based on a self-reflexive examination of the motives underlying my definition: a 'primary way of knowing based on our subjectivity or our being' where 'one's know-ledge and experience of the situation changes through being involved. There is not a significant separation between what one knows and what one is' (Rose 1997: 389). However, it would also be consistent with my basic thesis if other people adopted different perspectives. Having said this, I hope that my two viewpoints will have some resonance with others' experiences.

## Attempts to define counselling

There have, in recent years, been several attempts to define and distinguish counselling from other professions that use an element of talk in their therapeutic practice. Such attempts, moreover, have tended to identify three broad categories of talking therapy. The first category comprises those interventions that are sophisticated in regard to their non-talking aspects, but basic in regard to their use of counselling technique, for example, psychiatry, clinical psychology and advice work. Psychiatry is sophisticated as a medical intervention and as a diagnostic practice, but does not, as such, require any in-depth training in counselling; clinical psychology is sophisticated in the use of psychological testing but basic as a counselling method and, like psychiatry, does not involve any in-depth training in the methods of the talking cure. Advice work, meanwhile, requires a wealth of knowledge about different areas of life – finance, careers, and so on – but only a basic knowledge of counselling technique. The secondly category is counselling itself, or what I will later refer to as clinical counselling. Finally, there are those interventions which are perceived as being more in-depth since their training in the technique of the talking therapy is intense and protracted, namely psychotherapy and psychoanalysis.

The founders of the primary counselling organization in the United Kingdom, the British Association for Counselling (the BAC), decided to 'encompass as wide a range of interests in counselling as possible' (Bond 1989: 3) when they formed the new organization. In so doing they were careful about its name. If they had, for example, called it the British Association for Counsellors they would have excluded, by implication, the other categories of psychological intervention that I have mentioned, since it would have been an organization 'for counsellors' as opposed to being an organization 'for counselling' in general (Bond 1989). Having done this, however, the broadly based nature of the BAC has brought its own problems. There has been a certain degree of confusion about the precise nature of counselling and, even worse, the BAC has laid itself open to media claims of low standards of membership. So, in order to maintain standards of practice of counselling proper, the BAC has additionally made a clear distinction between counselling and the more basic counsel-ling interventions – between counselling and what is known as 'counselling skills'. The BAC Code of Ethics and Practice, for example, states that when a counsellor and client 'explicitly agree to enter into a counsel-ling relationship' it can be described as '"counselling" rather than the use of "counselling skills"' (BAC 1996: 3.2). The distinction is made more explicit by having separate codes of ethics and practice for the two disciplines.

Having established clear distinctions between counselling and coun-selling skills, the BAC made no distinction between counselling and the more so-called 'in-depth' therapies. The Code of Ethics and Practice, for example, states that 'it is not possible to make a generally accepted distinction between counselling and psychotherapy' (BAC 1996: 3.3). However, in contrast to this, many practitioners do make a distinction. Indeed, there has been a steady stream of articles debating whether there is a distinction or not and, if so, how such a distinction can be made (for example, Conyers 1988; Einzig 1989; Thorne 1992; Noonan 1993; McLeod 1993; Naylor-Smith 1994, and Jacobs 1994).

Conyers, Einzig, and Naylor-Smith, whilst recognizing the value of counselling, all seem to take it for granted that psychotherapy is a more sophisticated activity. Conyers (1988) speaks of counselling addressing the symptom and psychotherapy addressing the root cause, of counselling concentrating on the 'conscious overt dialogue' and psychotherapy 'working through former conflicts and neuroses through the mechanism of transference, resistance, dreamwork, etc, with the therapist' (29). Einzig (1989) and Naylor-Smith (1994) draw similar distinctions. Einzig sees psychotherapy as deeper, as tending to work more with the past and with the unconscious, and as working more with the dynamics of the therapeutic relationship itself, whilst Naylor-Smith sees the distinction in terms of different foci, although his view essentially amounts to the same. In counselling the focus is on 'life "out there"', whilst psychotherapy focuses on 'the unconscious, dreams, phantasy, the transference and counter-transference, and the relationship of all this to the client's personal history and to present problems' (285). Indeed, he goes further by establishing a distinction between counselling, psychodynamic counselling, psychotherapy, and psychoanalysis. This viewpoint is also adopted by Noonan (1993), who places psychoanalytic counselling in a hierarchy below psychoanalysis and psychoanalytic psychotherapy and above other forms of counselling, on the grounds that psychoanalytic counselling is 'more powerful, more inclusive, more demanding than any of the schools which came into being as splinters of psychoanalysis: Person-centred, Transactional Analysis, Gestalt, Primal Scream, and so on' (20). In conclusion one could say that these practitioners all, in one way or another, distinguish counselling from psychotherapy on the basis of such factors as depth, intensity, frequency of sessions, and duration of contracts.

McLeod (1993: 2) essentially adopts the same perspective. Whilst acknowledging that some practitioners make no distinction at all, he states that 'one significant difference . . . is that much counselling is conducted by non-professional volunteer workers, whereas psychotherapy is an excusively professional organization' (2), thus coming down on the side of those that make a distinction. Thorne (1992), in contrast, speaking out of the person-centred tradition, presents the view that psychotherapy and counselling are essentially the same and points out that many authors, including Carl Rogers, have used the terms interchangeably. He suggests that attempts to establish differences arise out of such human weaknesses as 'prestige, professional power . . . earning capacity . . . survival of the fittest' (246). Jacobs (1994), however, adopts a less clear cut perspective. First of all he points out that the debate is essentially one that is the concern of therapists working psychodynamically or psychoanalytically, 'since most of the other prinicipal orientations . . . see the two terms either as co-terminous, and therefore interchangeable, or as subsumed under the one term "therapy"' (80) – thereby, in a sense, confirming Thorne's view. Second, he makes the point that some therapists are 'open to the idea of a continuum between counselling and therapy . . . a middle position, where a practitioner may function as either or both' (81). In other words, a counsellor can sometimes work psychotherapeutically and a psycho-therapist can sometimes switch into counsellor mode. Finally, he comes to the conclusion that many of the conventional ways of making a distinction – such as length of contract, 'depth' and working with the 'transference' – are inadequate and, instead, tries to establish similarities and differences on the basis of a series of constructs or criteria which can be used to explore both similarities and differences.

In conclusion, the literature suggests that there is general agreement about the counselling–counselling skills distinction, but less agreement about the counselling–psychotherapy distinction. Some see a clear distinction whilst others, including the BAC, make no clear distinction. What, if anything, can the primary knowing perspective add to these perspectives?

## Primary observation of counselling theory and practice

In my career as a counsellor I initially trained, and then worked, with practitioners who were psychodynamically or psychoanalytically orientated. What was interesting about this experience, in retrospect, was that other viewpoints paled into insignificance and seemed irrelevant and inferior. I developed the sense that psychodynamic counselling was superior to other forms of counselling, but inferior to psychoanalytic psychotherapy and psychoanalysis. I thus tended to adopt a hierarchical approach to counselling, like some of the practitioners already quoted. However, since then I have worked in several settings with practitioners from most other theoretical orientations and studied different counselling theories for the purposes of teaching, and have been surprised at the extent to which my views have changed – including my 'definition' of counselling. The profession is much richer than I imagined – full of interesting and stimulating ideas and techniques – and I have been less inclined to establish distinctions and definitions based on a hierarchy of theories and techniques. Still more recently I have worked clinically with some goal- and solution-orientated therapists and within an academic environment, with colleagues who emphasize research and evaluation, and have come to value these viewpoints to a greater extent than before. Once again, this has resulted in a basic revision of my 'definition'. It has reinforced my tendency to see the value of a broad variety of interventions – to see them as complementary rather than superior or inferior to each other.

My view about these different theoretical outlooks has clearly changed depending on where I am. Now this may be due to the fact that I am an extremely fickle person. It is probably due, in any case, to a natural process of professional development and to changes in professional thinking generally. Indeed, there is a current of opinion today which recognizes the value of different viewpoints and which has been referred to as a 'cultural anthropological' stance. When confronted with different theories such practitioners adopt a position of 'surprise, curiosity, excitement, enthusiasm, sympathy' (Schweder, cited in Safran & Messer 1997: 141) – as opposed to 'an attitude of superiority, contempt and aversion' – which is precisely what I have tended to do as I have discovered different theoretical approaches. However, perhaps it also has something to do with deep-seated aspects of human nature – a possibility which I will now examine from a psychoanalytical point of view.

Psychoanalytic theory stresses, amongst other things, the power and importance of human relationships – indeed it goes as far as saying that our personality structure is determined by our human environment, or early object relations. Although relating primarily to childhood, this principle can be extended to any human situation, including the different professional milieus that I have described. In psychoanalytic terms my attitudes were influenced by the interactions I had with my immediate colleagues as a result of a process of introjection, identification and projection. I internalized the attitudes of others and they impacted on me in such a way that my perception of other practitioners became distorted. I identified with a succession of trainers, peers and colleagues and, to some extent, introjected their values and beliefs. Meanwhile, I projected all sorts of negative viewpoints on other theories which were, in effect, subjectively coloured impressions rather than accurate observations. In the early days my perspective on practitioners from other theoretical persuasions was fragmentary, limited and distorted – and tended to see different theoretical perspectives in terms of good and bad. In Kleinian terms it contained elements of the paranoid-schizoid position. But, through contact with people from other persuasions and outlooks, I developed a more complete, tolerant and realistic view of these other theories, and moved on to the Kleinian depressive position. I developed a more pluralistic postmodern outlook based on my training and subsequent professional development and experience.

## Conclusion: what is clinical counselling in context?

Attempts to define counselling and distinguish it from other talking therapies have resulted in a variety of viewpoints, ranging from those which have concluded that it is clearly distinct from other talking therapies, to those which have concluded that there is no clear distinction. My primary experience, meanwhile, which I looked at in the light of object-relations theory, suggests yet another viewpoint. In attempting to come to a definition of clinical counselling in context I will thus keep these different perspectives in mind.

My definition of clinical counselling has two parts. The term 'clinical counselling' distinguishes counselling, as a professional activity with a therapeutic intent, from a counselling-skills activity in which the therapeutic activity is secondary to another professional activity. The description 'in context', meanwhile, distinguishes it from such forms of talking therapy as psychotherapy. Instead of making the distinction on the basis of depth, length of contract, and so on, as is usually the case, it is made on the basis of its contextual nature. Counsellors, by virtue of the fact that they are usually exposed to a whole range of contextual factors in the organizations in which they work, are able to build up a degree of expertise which arises out of their capacity to understand how the context affects the work. They are, so to speak, experts in working with all the issues that arise from the interface of organizational, social, cultural, political and clinical issues.

Reflecting on this definition from the point of view of my primary experience, moreover, suggests that such an objective definition is driven by unconscious introjective and projective processes, and is thus subjective. So what is the subjective agenda for my objective definition? Yet, on further reflection, these changes of perspective have suited my purposes well. At the moment, for example – in view of the fact that I am registered as a counsellor and not as a psychotherapist – it is in my interests to subvert the generally accepted hierarchy by imposing my own. Thereby I have defined counselling as superior to counselling skills activities, but also, as regards its contextual nature, as superior to psychotherapy. My definition thus contains an element of self-interest. Yet I would argue that the same applies to any definition.

These principles can also be applied to clinical work. Just as there are definitions of counselling, so there are ground rules for clinical practice, such as set times and no third-party involvement (see, for example, Warburton 1995). If a session is interrupted, or if a therapist fails to start a session on time or overruns slightly then, irrespective of any practical considerations, we are breaking the ground rules – or the frame – and this, as many people have observed (e.g. Warburton 1995; Hoag 1992), may be detrimental to the therapeutic process. Every practitioner should thus have the ability to work to a strict framework, even under pressure (and developing this skill should form a part of counselling training). Having said this, however, perhaps such techniques (indeed any technique) also contain a self-serving subjective aspect which we could usefully self-reflexively analyze. From the point of view of clinical practice, the term 'clinical counselling in context' would therefore suggest that, as practitioners, we develop the capacity to place our work on a solid basis of clinical theory and practice adopting, if necessary, a fixed clinical stand-point, but that we also become self-reflective in regard to our motives for adopting our clinical standpoint. We can then also become skilful in adapting to the vagaries and uniqueness of the context (with the proviso that we do this within the framework of our Code of Ethics and Practice). We work to strict rules and clinical practices, which we maintain or not depending on the needs of the situation (see Lees 1997 for a discussion of this).

# References

Appignanesi, L. (ed.) (1989), *Postmodernism*, London: Free Association Books.

Arlow, J.A. (1984), 'Psychoanalysis', in R.Corsini (ed.), *Current Psychotherapies*, Ithaca: Peacock.

Bergin, A.E. (1971), 'The evaluation of therapeutic outcomes', in A.E. Bergin and S.L. Garfield (eds), *Handbook of Psychotherapy and Behavior Change*, New York: Wiley.

Bond, T. (1989), 'Towards defining the role of counselling skills', *Counselling*, 69: 3–11.

British Association for Counselling (1996), *Code of Ethics and Practice for Counsellors*, Rugby: British Association for Counselling.

Clarkson, P. (1996), 'Researching the "therapeutic relationship" in psychoanalysis, counselling psychology and psychotherapy: a quantitative enquiry', *Counselling Psychology Quarterly*, 9(2): 143–162.

Conyers, M. (1988), 'Counselling into psychotherapy: a change of emphasis', *Counselling*, 66: 27–31.

Corney, R. (1997), 'A Counsellor in every General Practice?' Inaugural lecture, 6 March 1997, London: The University of Greenwich.

Einzig, H. (1989), *Counselling and Psychotherapy: Is It For Me?*, Rugby: British Association for Counselling.

Ellenberger, H.F. (1970), *The Discovery of the Unconscious*, New York: Basic Books.

Eysenck, H.J. (1952), 'The effects of psychotherapy: an evaluation', *Journal of Consulting Psychology*, 16: 319–324.

Gordon, R. (1993), *Bridges*, London: Karnac Books.

Guntrip, H. (1973), *Psychoanalytic Theory, Therapy and the Self*, New York: Basic Books.

Hill, C.E. and Corbett, M.M. (1993), 'A perspective on the history of process and outcome research in counseling psychology', *Journal of Counseling Psychology*, 40(1): 3–24.

Hoag, L. (1992), 'Psychotherapy in the general practice surgery', *British Journal of Psychotherapy*, 8(4): 417–429.

House, R. and Totton, N. (1997), *Implausible Professions: Arguments for Pluralism and Autonomy in Psychotherapy and Counselling*, Ross-on-Wye, UK: PCCS Books.

Jacobs, M. (1994), 'Psychodynamic counselling: an identity achieved?', *Psychodynamic Counselling*, 1(1): 79–93.

Lees, J. (1997), 'An approach to counselling in GP surgeries', *Psychodynamic Counselling*, 3(1): 33–48.

Lynch, G. (1996), 'What is truth? A philosophical introduction to counselling research', *Counselling*, 7(2): 144–149.

—— (1997), 'The Oedipus complex in the work of Sigmund Freud and Heinz Kohut: a postmodern critique', *Psychodynamic Counselling*, 3(4): 371–387.

McLeod, J. (1993), *An Introduction to Counselling*, Buckingham, UK: Open University Press.

McRobbie, A. (1989), 'Postmodernism and popular culture', in L. Appignanesi (ed.), *Postmodernism*, London: Free Association Books, 165–179.

Meehl, P.E. (1997), 'Credentialed persons, credentialed knowledge', *Clinical Psychology: Science and Practice*, 4(2): 91–98.

Naylor-Smith, A. (1994), 'Counselling and psychotherapy: is there a difference?', *Counselling*, 5(4): 284–286.

Noonan, E. (1993), 'Tradition in training', in L. Spurling (ed.), *From the Words of My Mouth*, London: Routledge, 18–39.

Rose, K. (1997), 'Counselling as a product or a process?', *Psychodynamic Counselling*, 3(4): 387–401.

Safran, J.D. and Messer, S.B. (1997), 'Psychotherapy integration: a postmodern critique', *Clinical Psychology: Science and Practice*, 4(2): 140–152.

Samuels, A. (1989), *The Plural Psyche*, London: Routledge.

Stevens, A. (1990), *On Jung*, Harmondsworth, UK: Penguin Books.

Thorne, B. (1992), 'Psychotherapy and counselling: the quest for differences', *Counselling*, 3(4): 244–248.

Warburton, K. (1995), 'Student counselling: a consideration of framework and ethical issues', *Psychodynamic Counselling*, 1(3): 421–437.

# Acknowledgement

Scripture quotation taken from the Holy Bible, New International Version. Copyright © 1973, 1978, 1984 by International Bible Society. Used by permission of Hodder & Stoughton Ltd. All rights reserved.

'NIV' is a registered trademark of International Bible Society. UK trademark number 1448790.

# 2 A pragmatic approach to clinical counselling in context

*Gordon Lynch*

In this chapter we will think about two particular philosophical perspectives from which we can approach counselling theory and practice. The first of these is positivism. Positivism is a philosophical framework closely associated with traditional methods of scientific enquiry, and as such has been influential on the work of psychoanalytical, behaviourist and even client-centred therapists who have sought to maintain an objective view of their work. The second of these perspectives is pragmatism, which has tended up to this point to be less influential in the human sciences than the positivist approach.

I want to argue here that pragmatism is a more promising philosophical perspective for us as counsellors than positivism, particularly if we are committed to developing an approach to counselling which is contextually sensitive and which makes sense in a postmodern age. I also want to spend some time discussing what issues a pragmatic perspective specifically raises in relation to counselling.

This chapter might not seem very appealing to some readers, for if the technical talk here about positivism and pragmatism (both of which are explained further on) is not off-putting, serious doubts might remain as to the value of us thinking about this subject as counsellors. This kind of discussion is valuable, however, for increasing our awareness of the philosophical assumptions that we bring to our counselling work. These assumptions are strongly influential upon the way in which we practise as counsellors. For example, if I believe that the theory guiding my counselling work is absolutely true, then I will interact with my clients very differently than if I see the counselling theory that I use as simply one possible perspective amongst many. As we become more aware of the assumptions that influence our own counselling practice we have a greater opportunity to reflect on our work with clients and to become more thoughtful as practitioners. Even if, by the end of this chapter, you decide that your sympathies ultimately lie with neither the positivist nor the pragmatic perspective, the process of thinking about them will make you more aware of what assumptions and beliefs underpin your own counselling practice and provide you with new ways of reflecting about your work as a counsellor.

Initially in this chapter I will talk about the influence of positivism on the understanding of counselling and identify some of the key assumptions about the world that are made by positivism. I will then go on to explore some of the objections that can be made against these positivist assumptions, and to describe the alternative perspective of pragmatism. Finally, I will summarise some of the implications for our approach to counselling theory and practice if we adopt a pragmatic viewpoint.

## Positivism and the search for universal theories of therapy

> For many years I have been engaged in psychotherapy with individuals in distress. In recent years I have found myself increasingly concerned with the process of abstracting from that experience the general principles which appear to be involved in it. I have endeavored to discover any orderliness, any unity which seems to inhere in the subtle, complex tissue of interpersonal relationships in which I have so constantly been immersed in therapeutic work. One of the current products of this concern is an attempt to state, in formal terms, a theory of psychotherapy, of personality, and of interpersonal relationship which will encompass and contain the phenomena of my experience.
>
> (Rogers 1957: 95)

These are the opening sentences of one of the most significant articles in the field of counselling and psychotherapy in this century, Carl Rogers's 'The necessary and sufficient conditions of therapeutic personality change'. In this article Rogers sets out what have become known as the 'core conditions' of effective therapeutic relationships, and his ideas here have been influential not only for those who see themselves as person-centred counsellors but, more generally, on the wider counselling movement.

For the purposes of this chapter, however, I want to focus not on the content of what Rogers said in this article, but on what he was trying to do when he wrote it. As the opening lines of the article make clear, Rogers's aim in writing this piece was to develop a generalised theory of therapy based on his own experience of working with clients. Furthermore, in this article Rogers does not simply aim to offer his readers a theory, but to set out a hypothesis about the conditions for constructive personality change which could be tested in subsequent research. Indeed, Rogers even goes to the length of suggesting ways in which such research could appropriately be designed. Because such talk of hypotheses and research design is often of little interest to counsellors who see themselves as practitioners rather than researchers or academics, it is easy for readers to 'blank out' these parts of the article and to focus instead on the content of what Rogers was saying about the core conditions. To do this, however, is to miss an important dimension of what this article is about. For 'The necessary and sufficient conditions of therapeutic personality change' is important not only as a statement of the idea of the core conditions, but also as an example of the wider effort in this century to develop universal theories of counselling and psychotherapy.

The idea that it is helpful to try to develop theories of what makes counselling work across different times, places, settings and cultures may not seem a very controversial one to many people. The pioneering figures in the field of counselling and psychotherapy (e.g. Freud, Rogers, Skinner) have all tended to assume that if a therapeutic theory is true then it can be applied to client work regardless of when, where or with whom the therapy takes place. Indeed, if we could not be sure that the theory that informed our counselling work was true, then what authority would we have for our work with our clients? Such a theory might need to be complex to account for the different experiences we have with clients, but again, surely this does not mean it is impossible to have an adequate or true theory even if we feel that we are still only working towards defining it? If we do engage in the search for a universally applicable theory for our counselling work, then we are certainly in good company. The quest for a universal theory of counselling is still actively pursued by many today within individual 'schools' of therapeutic theory, just as it was pursued by Rogers back in the 1950s (see, e.g., Thorne 1991; Salkovskis 1996).

Whilst it is often assumed that the search for universally applicable theories of counselling and psychotherapy is a natural and useful pursuit, there are assumptions within this activity which merit further exploration. Indeed, the attempt to form such universal theories rests on a view of the world which has become increasingly controversial as this century has gone on.

Rogers's work in 'The necessary and sufficient conditions of therapeutic personality change', and the search for universal theories of therapy more generally, rest on assumptions about the world that derive from the philosophical perspective of positivism. Positivism was one expression of the movement in Western society from the eighteenth century onwards towards an emphasis on knowledge being based on scientific inquiry rather than theological dogma or philosophical reflection. First set out as a coherent perspective by Auguste Comte (1798–1857), positivism emphasised that our knowledge of the world should only be based on what we can observe (Leahey 1980). When sufficient numbers of observations about a particular phenomenon have been made, a generalised theory can be formed in relation to it, whose truth can be judged on the basis of its power in predicting what will happen in certain circumstances. Positivist researchers seek to develop theories about the world that are universally true, whilst recognising that the truth of a theory is always provisional and subject to it not being contradicted by subsequent observations (see Chalmers 1982; Gergen 1994b).

Central to the positivist viewpoint is the belief that there are certain universal 'facts' about the world and that the discovery of these facts is made possible through neutral and objective observation of the world. Indeed this belief is absolutely foundational to attempts to develop universal theories about what the world or human beings are like, for if there were no 'facts', or no objective way of discovering what the facts were, how could we hope to make a statement that was universally true? This belief in the existence of 'facts' and the possibility of objectively knowing them has become increasingly open to doubt as this century has gone on, however. In the next part of this chapter we will look at both academic and cultural sources of this doubt.

## Some problems with objectivity and truth

One of the major developments across a range of academic disciplines over the course of this century has been the increased attention that has been given to the role of language in relation to our knowledge of the world. For someone adopting a positivist view, language is opaque, simply a neutral means of communicating the 'facts' of the world that we know by our observations. Over the past decades, however, there have been a growing number of voices questioning this view of language and suggesting that, far from simply giving a neutral depiction of the world as it is, language actually constructs our view of the world (Gergen 1994a).

Two of the most important writers for the development of this alternative view of language have been the linguist Ferdinand de Saussure and the philosopher Ludwig Wittgenstein. Saussure introduced the distinction between the 'signifier' and the 'signified' in language (Saussure 1974). According to Saussure, the signifier was the word that was used in relation to an object and the signified was the object itself. Thus the word 'ball' is a signifier, of which the signifier is the round object that I can pick up, throw or kick around. Where Saussure began radically to change our understanding of language was in his proposal that the signifiers that we use in relation to the world are not straightforward labels for objects that everyone can see, but arbitrary ways of dividing up the world, and that different languages divide the world up in different ways.

This point becomes important if we recognise that we are unable to 'see' things for which we have no language. Take the example of someone taking a course in car maintenance. At the start of the course (if the person is a complete novice) the view under the car's bonnet will be a bewildering array of shapes, wires and tubes. As the course progresses, however, and the person finds out about the 'distributor', the 'alternator', the 'carburetter', and so on, they will begin to 'see' what is under the bonnet in a new way. Our ability to 'see' objects is thus dependent upon our having words for them, for until I have a word for a particular object I will not be able to see it distinctively in relation to other objects. If we accept Saussure's point that words are arbitrary ways of dividing up the world then it follows that the objects that we 'see' are a product of the language we use. Saussure thus introduced the idea that rather than simply giving us a neutral representation of the world as it actually is, our language shapes and limits what we are able to see in the world.

A related point was made by the philosopher Ludwig Wittgenstein in his later work (Wittgenstein 1963; see also Lynch 1996). Wittgenstein took issue with the idea that people are born with a universal, private language inside their heads and that a child learns to communicate by matching this private, inner language with the particular words that are used in its culture. Instead, Wittgenstein argued, all language is public and learning a language is a process of being trained into the particular linguistic rules and conventions of one's culture. The meanings of words therefore arise out of the way they are used by particular groups at particular times, and we are able to communicate with others only in so far as we stick to the rules of how to speak that operate in our culture. One of the main implications of Wittgenstein's argument here is that our view of the world is profoundly shaped by the words, phrases and linguistic rules of the particular communities in which we grow up. This, when, taken together with Saussure's views, suggests that far from being a neutral vehicle for our impressions of the world, language actually shapes and limits what we see in the world according to the conventions of our particular community and culture. We can thus begin to think about our views of the world as being socially constructed, a product of the language and concepts of our particular culture rather than an objective view of the world as it is.

It can be very challenging for us as counselling practitioners if we begin to apply some of these ideas to how we see our own work. For example, psychodynamic counsellors have traditionally worked on the basis that the unconscious is a real entity within an individual's psychological structure. The assumption here is that the word 'unconscious' is simply a label that can be attached to a phenomenon that is present in every individual. If we see language creating our view of the world, rather than simply representing it, however, then the 'unconscious' becomes a linguistic device, a way of talking about the world that helps us to see it in certain ways. Not only that, but it becomes a way of talking about the world that has been learnt through our being a part of a particular community, such as a psychodynamic counselling course or a psychoanalytic therapy group, or by our being exposed to psychodynamic culture through, for example, reading psychodynamic textbooks. Many counsellors work on the basis that their counselling theory gives some objective account of individual and group psychology. If we accept the arguments advanced by Saussure, Wittgenstein and others, however, it becomes more convincing to see the various counselling theories on offer as simply different ways of talking about the world that are maintained by different groups, whose truth can be neither proven nor disproven. Looking at counselling theory in this way could help us to understand how counsellors from different orientations can look at the same case study and yet see it in different ways, for, as we noted above, our ability to see the world rests first of all upon the language that we have been taught.

Whilst some counselling practitioners find these issues of language and our way of 'seeing' the world interesting and thought-provoking, others find this kind of discussion abstract, dry or divorced from real experience. Even if these academic arguments are dismissed as irrelevant, however, there are still strong social and cultural pressures in our day-to-day lives which make it harder for us to believe that we are able to possess some kind of objective knowledge of the ultimate truths of our existence (see Gergen 1991; Truett Anderson 1996). Foremost amongst these are the technological changes which have made global travel and communication easier than it was even thirty years ago. A recent advertising slogan for a telecommunications company was 'Geography is history', and there is a widespread sense of the world becoming a smaller place as more people travel by air, use the growing telephone network, communicate via e-mail and the Internet and receive images from around the world from ever-expanding media services.

Such is the degree of change within our current period of history that many commentators have given it a distinctive name, referring to it as 'postmodernity' (Best & Kellner 1991). It has been argued that a significant feature of postmodernity has been that as we have become increasingly exposed to other cultures and to other ways of looking at the world, we have become less sure that our own views represent the ultimate truth about reality and more open to the idea that our views are just one possible perspective amongst many. Beliefs that have been enshrined at the heart of Western culture, such as the Christian faith or the belief in reason and scientific progress, increasingly look like 'local' traditions rather than timeless or universal ways of understanding life (Doan & Parry 1994). Whilst some may seek to defend against this by retreating into fundamentalism, a significant feature of our time does indeed seem to be the growth of uncertainty. Thus, even if academic objections to the possibility of an objective knowledge of the world leave us cold or uninterested, we may well have a general sense that our views of life may not be as objective as previous generations have hitherto thought.

Two contrasting ways of understanding human knowledge have thus emerged out of our discussion so far. One is the positivist view, which emphasises the possibility of developing theories which are universally applicable across different situations and places. The other is a view, often now associated with the word 'postmodern', which emphasises that our knowledge of the world is always limited by the particular language and concepts of our culture, and is therefore always local and partial. The positivist view sees the means to discovering the 'facts' of the world as being objective observation of the world. The postmodern view is sceptical about the possibility of having an objective knowledge of facts about the world, because our way of seeing the world is always shaped by the particular time and culture within which we live. Indeed, postmodernists abandon any talk of there being discoverable 'facts' about the world, and focus instead on the way in which we use language to create and maintain our understanding of the world. If positivism is about trying to provide us with an accurate map of reality, postmodernism leaves us with an array of different, locally produced maps, with no means of knowing which is more accurate than another.

As counsellors this choice of ways of seeing the world can present us with a dilemma. The search for universal theories of counselling needs something like a positivist view of the world, with its belief in the possibility of an objective knowledge of the 'facts' of our existence. Such a positivist perspective is becoming increasingly difficult to maintain, however, for even if we find the arguments about language advanced by Wittgenstein and Saussure obscure or irrelevant, the experience of living through 'postmodernity' makes it harder for us to believe that any one person, group or theory can provide us with an objective account of the ultimate truths of our existence. Yet if we take on board a postmodern view of the world, where does that leave us as counsellors? If we can no longer be sure that our counselling theories are true or universally applicable, then what grounds do we have for sitting in front of clients as agents of support and healing? In the next part of this chapter, I want to suggest that the philosophical approach of pragmatism offers a promising way of preserving a postmodern scepticism about the possibility of knowing the ultimate truths of existence whilst also having a sense of the value of our counselling theories and of the work we do with our clients.

## Defining pragmatism

Up until now, an unexamined assumption within this discussion has been that the authority of particular counselling theories rests on the extent to which they give a true account of human existence. The chief criterion for assessing the adequacy of a counselling theory is thus, in this view, an examination of the theory's truthfulness. If it is problematic for us to think in terms of knowing the truth about our existence, however, what alternative ways might there be for us to think about our counselling theories and practice? A promising option, and the one to be explored in this chapter, is to think in terms not of the truthfulness of the ideas that inform our counselling work, but of their *usefulness* in achieving desirable outcomes for us and our clients.

An emphasis on looking at the usefulness of human knowledge has been at the centre of the philosophical approach of pragmatism, an approach which has been particularly influential in the United States and is associated with writers such as Charles Peirce, William James, and more recently Richard Rorty (see, e.g., Rorty 1991a). As a philosophical perspective, pragmatism is characterised by a view of knowledge not as 'a matter of getting reality right, but rather as a matter of acquiring habits of action for coping with reality' (Rorty 1991b: 1). In this view, truth is not something that we can, ultimately, attain – or as Rorty puts it 'truth is not the sort of thing one should expect to have a philosophically interesting theory about' (Stout 1988: 250). Rather, our focus should be on practical knowledge. A pragmatist, in this philosophical sense, thus emphasises the importance of 'knowing how to' perform a certain task to achieve a certain result rather than 'knowing that' a certain statement about reality is true.

Pragmatism therefore shares with postmodernism an aversion to talking about issues of truth and truthfulness. As a consequence, pragmatism is being seen by some people with postmodern sympathies as a useful way of looking at human knowledge. For example, the psychologist Donald Polkinghorne has argued for the value of what he calls 'neopragmatism' as a philosophical perspective for psychology and psychological therapies in the postmodern age. Polkinghorne describes 'neopragmatic' knowledge in the following way:

A neopragmatic body of knowledge consists of summary general-isations of which type of action has been successful in prior like situations. These summaries are always unfinished and are in need of continual revision as newly effective actions are discovered. Neo-pragmatism does not suppose these generalisations to be predictive of what actions will work in new situations; rather, the generalisations have only heuristic value as indicators of what might be tried in similar situations. Because neopragmatism incorporates the post-modern understanding of fragmentariness, it holds that each specific situation is different and contains the uncertainties of its specific location and time. Neopragmatism also holds to the notion of equifinality – that is, the same end can be accomplished in multiple ways. The determination of the value of an action depends on whether it fulfilled its purpose, not whether it followed a particular recipe.

(Polkinghorne 1992: 152)

The type of knowledge that Polkinghorne describes here is very different from a knowledge of reality that is held to be true at all times and in all places. What Polkinghorne proposes is that our knowledge is best seen not in terms of timeless truths, but in terms of what has worked in the past. As Polkinghorne points out, just because something has worked in the past does not mean that it will necessarily work again in another time and setting. Rather, we need to allow ourselves both to be informed by what we have found to work in the past, and to be open to the new possibilities and conditions of each new experience, to discovering afresh what works in each new context.

This approach might appear somewhat over-cautious to some readers. In many respects, however, it seems to capture important aspects of the experience of working with clients as a counsellor. For example, I might discover that it proves helpful with one client who expresses anxieties about relationships to focus on the transference and to explore what it means for them to feel anxious about being emotionally close to me in the therapeutic relationship. With another client who expresses similar anxieties about relationships, however, I might find that this approach is not fruitful and that it is actually much more useful simply to talk with them about their worries about a new friendship that they are developing. The factors influencing what works in these two different situations would include both my own and the client's style of relating to others, the client's expectations about the counselling, the client's resources for dealing with painful feelings, the setting in which we are working and the duration of the counselling relationship. Clearly no two counselling relationships will offer exactly the same combinations of each of these factors, and whilst we might find that there are some general principles which work well a reasonable amount of the time, there are good grounds for being open to the uniqueness of each individual counselling relationship.

A pragmatic view of counselling therefore casts doubt on the idea that we can develop particular ways of working with clients (e.g. simply offering the core conditions or responding to faulty patterns of thinking) that will work with all clients at all times. Rather, a pragmatic approach invites us to reflect on what has worked for clients in the past, but also on what might work with this particular client in this particular setting at this particular time.

A pragmatic perspective also raises the issues of what results or outcomes we are seeking for our clients, for different ways of working with them may well result in different outcomes. For example, a counsellor working in the occupational health department of a large company may be working with a client who is experiencing burnout after having been subjected to unrealistic workloads and active bullying from their manager. The counsellor might decide simply to teach this client stress-management techniques to help them deal with the distress of their working situation in a more effective way. Alternatively, the counsellor might decide to work with the client primarily to restore the client's self-esteem to the point where they feel able to make a formal complaint about their treatment at work. Or possibly the counsellor might decide to attempt to achieve both of these aims. The point is that the way in which the counsellor actually does work with this client is, consciously or unconsciously, influenced by the counsellor's own views about what would represent a positive outcome for the client. Our clients are likely to be better served if we are able to be more aware of some of these value choices, so that we can be more reflective in evaluating what represents good outcomes for our clients and what are the best ways of thinking about these issues.

In this chapter so far, two approaches to understanding counselling work have been set out. The first, underpinned by positivist assumptions, assumes that it is possible to develop a theory of counselling which is universally true and which can be usefully applied with all clients, at all times and in all places. The second, informed by pragmatism, focuses much more on what sort of actions are useful in achieving certain ends and recognises that what works differs depending on the time and context in which one acts. The first of these approaches has, to date, been the dominant way of approaching counselling theory and practice. As we move into a new century and a new millennium it seems likely that increasing amounts of attention will be given to the second approach, if only because this more humble and contextually sensitive approach rings true with our experience of living in an age of fragmentation and uncertainty. Although not all the contributors to this book will wholeheartedly agree with this second approach, it does represent a viable philosophical perspective from which the book's emphasis on the importance of context for our counselling work can be understood.

## Implications of a pragmatic approach to counselling

If we choose to adopt pragmatism as the philosophical perspective that informs our counselling work, then what are the implications of this for our views of counselling theory and practice? This is clearly a subject for ongoing discussion, but I would make the following suggestions.

First, a pragmatic approach emphasises the importance of counselling theory in enabling us to be 'present' to our clients and in helping us to work with them to make sense of their experience. In this chapter so far we have explored the idea that it is not possible for us to have an understanding of the ultimate 'facts' of reality and that, as a consequence, it is not possible for us to know whether our counselling theories give us a knowledge of the truths of human existence. This idea might be seen to call into question the value of having counselling theories at all, for if we cannot know whether or not these theories are true, why seek to develop or maintain them? I would agree that if the only function that counselling theories play is to attempt to offer truthful accounts of the world, then their value would indeed seem to be questionable. But I would also suggest that counselling theories can be seen as having a usefulness for us as practitioners, regardless of these issues about their truth.

For example, counselling theory performs an important role in enabling the counsellor simply to *be* with the client as the counselling process develops. The experience of sitting with clients who may be experiencing terrible pain, anxiety or confusion can be very difficult for the counsellor. This experience is more tolerable, however, if the counsellor has some theoretical framework that helps them to make sense for themselves of the client's distress and gives them some idea of how they might usefully respond to their client. Equally, counselling theory can be beneficial in helping clients to understand their experience. In a review of literature describing what clients value about therapy, David Howe (1993) noted that one of the key things that clients value is that their therapist 'talks with them' to help them to make sense of events or feelings that have been significant in bringing them to counselling. If applied sensitively and appropriately, counselling theories may guide the counsellor's conversation with their client so that the client is helped to understand their experience in ways that are new, helpful and satisfying. Thus, irrespective of issues of their truthfulness, counselling theories have the potential to help counsellors bear their clients' distress and to work with them to make sense of it.

Second, a pragmatic approach encourages us to think about our counselling practice in terms of what is useful and effective for particular clients within the contexts in which we work. If pragmatism encourages us to be sceptical about the notion of theories that are universally and timelessly true, and to focus instead on what works in particular contexts and cases, then this has clear implications for our counselling practice. For if confidence in the ultimate truth of our therapeutic approach is questionable, our counselling practice becomes not so much the rigid application of techniques or approaches that are prescribed by our particular therapeutic models but rather, a specific response to the uniqueness of the experience of this particular client in this particular setting at this particular time. Such an understanding of counselling practice highlights the need for sensitivity, thoughtfulness and creativity on the part of counsellors as they work with their clients. The development of these qualities within the counsellor is an important focus both for counsellor training and for supervision, with the proper goal of these activities being the counsellor's development of a sophisticated ability to reflect on what they are doing. This capacity for reflection has been described by Casement (1985) as an 'internal supervisor' and includes both the counsellor's awareness of their own thoughts, feelings and concerns and an awareness of the effects of their words and actions upon their client. Practitioner expertise, from this viewpoint, is less about abstract knowledge of particular theories and techniques and more about a thoughtful, skilful and timely approach to working with clients.

Each of these points about counselling theory and practice forms a necessary counterbalance to the other. An emphasis on the usefulness of counselling theories without a recognition of the importance of sensitivity, flexibility and thoughtfulness in their application runs the risk of leading to rigid, impersonal forms of counselling practice which fail to attend to what would be useful in the work with this particular client at this particular time and place. Similarly, an emphasis on flexibility and creativity in counselling practice which lacks a grounding in a theoretical framework runs the risk of promoting situations in which the counsellor feels swamped by the strong feelings that both they and the client experience during sessions. A pragmatic approach to counselling is, therefore, one which sees the usefulness both of counselling theory and of the flexible and situationally sensitive application of that theory.

## Summary

In this chapter I have briefly set out two different philosophical approaches that lead to different views of counselling theory and practice. I have suggested that the positivist approach, with its belief in observable 'facts' about human existence, has been influential in the way that counselling has been understood for much of this century. The positivist view of the world has become more problematic, however, as the idea that language constructs our view of the world has gained ground in academic circles. Furthermore, the experience of living in contemporary society typically increases our awareness of other views of the world and makes it harder for us to believe that our own views represent the ultimate truth. In this situation, pragmatism seems to offer a more fruitful and less problematic philosophical perspective for counselling work. With its emphasis on the *usefulness* rather than the *truthfulness* of our knowledge, pragmatism focuses our attention as counsellors on what works in promoting positive outcomes for particular clients in particular times and places. Pragmatism also encourages reflection about what we see as positive outcomes for our work with our clients. Within a pragmatic approach to counselling, it is helpful to emphasise both the importance of counselling theory in making our experience of being with clients easier to bear and understand, and the importance of the counsellor's ability to utilise theory in ways that are flexible, creative and thoughtful. The main focus of this chapter has been at the level of the assumptions and beliefs that shape the way we understand counselling. Even so, it has become clear that the pragmatic perspective outlined here raises more specific questions about the influence of our context upon our counselling work and about what works in producing positive outcomes for clients, given the uniqueness of each counselling relationship. This chapter therefore stands as an invitation to further discussion and reflection about the theory and practice of counselling at a range of different levels.

## References

Best, S. & Kellner, D. (1991) *Post-Modern Theory: Critical Interrogations.* Basingstoke: Macmillan.

Casement, P. (1985) *On Learning From the Patient.* London: Tavistock.

Chalmers, A. (1982) *What Is This Thing Called Science?.* Milton Keynes: Open University Press.

Doan, R. & Parry, A. (1994) *Story Re-Visions: Narrative Therapy in the Postmodern World.* New York: Guilford.

Gergen, K. (1991) *The Saturated Self.* New York: Basic Books.

Gergen, K. (1994a) *Realities and Relationships: Soundings in Social Constructionism.* Cambridge, MA: Harvard University Press.

Gergen, K. (1994b) *Towards Transformation in Social Knowledge* (2nd edition). London: Sage.

Howe, D. (1993) *On Being a Client: Understanding the Process of Counselling and Psychotherapy.* London: Sage.

Leahey, J. (1980) *A History of Psychology: Main Concepts in Psychological Thought.* Englewood Cliffs, New Jersey: Prentice-Hall.

Lynch, G. (1996) 'Words and silence: counselling and psychotherapy after Wittgenstein', *Counselling*, 8(2), 126–128.

Polkinghorne, D. (1992) 'Postmodern epistemology of practice', in (ed.) Kvale, S. *Psychology and Postmodernism.* London: Sage, 146–165.

Rogers, C. (1957) 'The necessary and sufficient conditions of therapeutic personality change', *Journal of Consulting Psychology*, 21, 95–103.

Rorty, R. (1991a) *Consequences of Pragmatism.* New York: Harvester/Wheatsheaf.

Rorty, R. (1991b) *Objectivity, Relativism and Truth.* Cambridge: Cambridge University Press.

Salkovskis, P. (ed.) (1996) *Frontiers of Cognitive Therapy.* New York: Guilford.

Saussure, F. de (1974) *Course in General Linguistics.* Glasgow: Fontana/Collins.

Stout, J. (1988) *Ethics after Babel: The Language of Morals and their Discontents.* Cambridge: James Clarke & Co.

Thorne, B. (1991) *Person-Centred Counselling: Therapeutic and Spiritual Dimensions.* London: Whurr.

Truett Anderson, W. (ed.) (1996) *The Fontana Post-Modernism Reader.* London: Fontana.

Wittgenstein, L. (1963) *Philosophical Investigations.* Oxford: Blackwell.

# 3 Assessment of psychological change and the future practice of clinical counselling

*Adrian Hemmings*

In this chapter I explore some of the reasons why we should attempt to research into counselling and describe the difficulties posed by attempting to measure psychological change. I describe how these difficulties have been addressed and consider the main types of research questions that have been posed. I continue by giving a brief history of outcome research of psychological therapies, in particular research which asks whether psychological interventions work. I then examine the implications of the research literature in today's evidence-based environment.

I finish by exploring the future of clinical counselling in the light of research and the movement towards a form of service provision called managed care.

## Why bother with research?

Many would say that what we do as counsellors is an art and not a science (Storr 1979). Counselling is a creative and intuitive activity and what happens between the practitioner and client is so subtle and includes so many variables, how can we possibly attempt to measure this activity with a degree of accuracy? The answer to this is that we probably can't. Our attempts to measure change are inevitably going to be crude, but that does not mean that we should not attempt to do so. There are several cogent arguments as to why we should conduct research in counselling. They come from three different sources: ethics, research evidence and pragmatism.

It can be argued that it is unethical to conduct an activity for which no attempt has been made to assess whether it works. This argument states that we owe it to our clients to attempt to monitor our and their progress and identify particular strategies which are effective and relinquish those that are not. Having a knowledge of procedures that have been shown to be effective enables the practitioner to make an informed choice within the context of the individual case. It is argued that as part of good practice we do this anyway. However, we tend not to in any formal way or in a way that is accessible to our clients and other bodies such as employers or funders. Some might say that too much monitoring affects the counselling relationship; besides, a competent practitioner should be able to rely on clinical judgement gained from years of experience. But what is the evidence that clinical judgement is as accurate as we think it is? This brings us to the second argument, research evidence.

Sadly, research has demonstrated time and time again that there are problems with relying solely on clinical judgement (Dawes 1986). This does not apply solely to counselling (Tverski & Kahnerman 1974). Clinical judgement has faired very poorly compared to other less complex models such as the statistical technique called regression. Experience does not fare much better and it has been shown that it is not necessarily a guarantee of better clinical outcomes. Several studies have demonstrated that trainee counsellors have achieved as good an outcome (in some studies better) than their more experienced colleagues, except when working with clients with more enduring problems (Crits-Christoph et al. 1991).

The third argument comes from a more pragmatic source, that of funding. There is an increasing trend for organisations that fund counselling to do so only for interventions that are evidence based. Lack of evidence does not necessarily mean that an intervention does not work, but this argument does not sit very easily with a funder who has limited resources for which there is considerable competition.

So if research into clinical counselling is going to take place, how can psychological change be measured?

## The nature of psychological change

Empirical science is based on accurate measurement. When this is undertaken in the natural sciences, e.g. physics, measurement is relatively straightforward. There is a clearly defined subject–object divide and most measurement can be undertaken by machine, thereby ensuring greater objectivity (Rennie 1994).

The study of humans is different. When humans study other humans, the subject–object divide is no longer clearly defined. As humans, the bulk of our activity is communicative and therefore we tend to attach meaning to other humans' behaviour: because of this we are aware of our effect on others and of others on us. In short, we are continually assessing, interpreting, measuring and affecting other people. This invites two questions: How can this information be broken down in terms that others can understand? How can it be broken down in a more formal way so that what we do can be taught to others?

In order to answer these questions we must first develop a model for the measurement of psychological change, preferably one that is itself dynamic. It must answer the questions of what we should measure, how we should measure it and from whom we shall take these measurements.

## Models of measurement

Lambert et al. (1991) have produced such a model and they convert the questions above into content, technology and source. 'Content' refers to what we are going to attempt to measure. The second category is 'technology', in other words, once we have decided what we are going to attempt to measure, how are we going to do this? The third dimension is 'source', in other words, from whom are we going to elicit this information? Each of these categories can be further divided into hierarchies and Lambert and colleagues have devised a chart that illustrates this (see Figure 3.1).

### Content

The hierarchy of content consists of three levels: (1) intrapersonal, such as self concept, psychopathology; (2) interpersonal, such as interpersonal problems, sexual performance; and (3) behavioural change and social adjustment. All are clearly relevant in the context of counselling. Social role performance, such as performance at work, is perhaps less relevant to counselling goals (Strupp & Hadley 1977). For example, a person who is

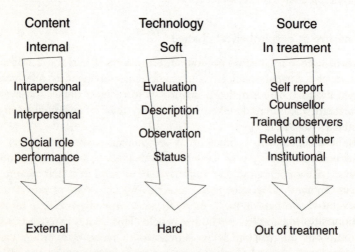

*Figure 3.1*  The Lambert model of psychological measurement
*Source:* Lambert et al. 1991

effective at work and yet still deeply unhappy may be deemed by their employer to have improved but would probably not be described as improved by either themselves or their counsellor.

## Technology

The hierarchy in this dimension can be said to describe a level of experimental rigour. Lambert et al. (1991) put evaluation at the 'soft' end of the hierarchy. Here 'soft' means that many of the controls (such as randomising and using specific interventions or measures) that are put into place in a research design are missing. Evaluation may include gross ratings of improvement by clients and counsellors. Interviews carried out by researchers are probably the most common form of simple evaluation, although there are a number of difficulties with this procedure. If there is to be any degree of uniformity in the way in which the information is elicited, then extensive training of interviewers is required. There is a danger that unstructured interviews may simply reflect the concerns of the interviewer rather than the interviewee. The presence of an interviewer may have an effect on information received about subjects that are socially sensitive, such as problems with sex. They are also time consuming and require a great deal of time and resources to process (Heppner et al. 1992).

The advantage of interviews is that they can be tailored to the individual and so can reflect information that is particular to them and their circumstances (Kerlinger 1986). They can also go to much greater depth and tap into more detailed information than other methods, and are most closely related to counselling: a good interviewer often has similar skills to those of a competent counsellor, making the transition from practice to research less daunting for a counselling practitioner who wishes to evaluate their own and others' work.

'Description', next in the hierarchy, allows for more uniform but less detailed individual information to be taken than the categories before it. Psychometric measures come into this category and the number of these available is vast (Buros 1978; Kline 1993; Ogles et al. 1990). They are by far the most commonly used forms of psychological measurement.

Practical considerations in administering a test need to be taken into account. In order to increase its accuracy a test may have an optimum number of items (Kline 1986), which can result in a lengthy test if there are several subscales. A client who is asked to complete several lengthy questionnaires may well become anxious (known as evaluation apprehension, Cook & Campbell 1979), which in turn may affect the validity of the measures. A careful balance between theory and practice needs to be struck.

Observation adds another dimension, and this usually entails the use of external observers who are specifically brought in for the study. However, observers need to have extensive training and are usually experts in the field, so may well add expense to the study. They may bring with them a wealth of experience and expertise but problems with individual ways of scoring may also occur (Orlinski & Howard 1978). The use of observers may be also be intrusive and may increase the participant's awareness of being researched and so alter their behaviour (known as the halo effect, Cook & Campbell 1979).

The physiological status of the client can be measured using a variety of instruments, such as blood pressure gauges and peripheral temperature monitors. This form of measurement is perhaps the most 'removed' form of inquiry. However, although physiological measures may be used in a study with a specific target symptom such as anxiety, their use is limited in counselling research.

## Source

The source of the data is ordered according to the level of participation in the treatment. The client is considered to be the most involved in the treatment and so might be considered the most relevant source of information. However, client self-ratings do have their limitations. Clients may be affected by their present mood (Beck et al. 1979), by the act of completing a form, by experimenter expectancies (Freidman 1967; Kazdin 1980) and by the counsellor (Hurvitz 1970). They may have limited access to their own thoughts and feelings or they may be prone to wanting to portray themselves in the most positive light (Orne & Wender 1968). All these issues need to be taken into account when choosing a way of measuring change.

As a source of rating, counsellors are also open to bias, through their assumptions and personal values (Abramowitz & Dockecki 1977; Rosenthal & Rosnow 1969). There is also evidence that, in general, counsellors tend to rate outcome more positively than clients or external observers (Bergin 1971). There are practical difficulties in asking counsellors to rate their clients, not least that of confidentiality.

Trained observers come next in the hierarchy. Although providing another facet to the data collected, there are several difficulties in using them which have already been commented upon.

Relevant others, such as spouse, friend or work colleague, once again give an added dimension to the data. They have been used extensively in the larger studies (Lieberman, Yalom & Miles 1973; Sloane et al. 1975).

However, there are practical problems in contacting relevant others, obtaining permission from the client and in the fact that some clients may not have relevant others, thus biasing the sample.

Institutional sources such as crime statistics or recorded substance misuse may be helpful when focusing on specific problems, but their relevance is questionable when global improvement is being measured.

A study with considerable resources at its disposal might incorporate a large proportion of these different categories in order to gain an in-depth view of outcome (e.g. the Second Sheffield Psychotherapy Project, Shapiro et al. 1994). However, more modest studies (i.e most studies) have to decide to make a choice of which combinations need to be used and on what grounds. Qualitative research which explores more individual in-depth issues is increasingly used in counselling research, either integrated into the quantitative work as a way of giving it more meaning, or as the main form of enquiry. By far the most common form of research in counselling continues to be the use of psychometric questionnaires for self-completion, with other forms of measurement added according to the resources available. It is this form of research that is described below.

## The questions asked in counselling research

Outcome research in counselling and psychotherapy has a history going back over sixty years. During this period the main questions asked of the research have changed. What was relevant in the 1950s is not so relevant today, as research has developed and built on previous knowledge. Unsurprisingly, the questions asked have become more sophisticated and complex. Lambert et al. (1991) provide a very useful framework in which to place the literature review by the type of research questions that are asked. They identify three main classes of research question:

1   Class I: does counselling work? (i.e. effectiveness questions);
2   Class II: if it is effective, are there any particular components which account for its effectiveness? (i.e. which model of counselling is most effective?);
3   Class III: if these components can be identified how can they be improved? (i.e. enhancement questions).

There is insufficient space in this chapter to summarise all three classes of research so I will give a brief resume of Class I: does counselling work?

## A history of studies that have addressed effectiveness questions

The history of studies that attempted to answer the effectiveness question can be roughly divided into three periods. The first period was between 1930 and 1952, before Eysenck's criticisms of psychotherapy and psychoanalysis were first published in a paper in 1952. This paper was mentioned in chapter 1 and its effect is considered again in this chapter. The second period was from Eysenck's paper until the development of meta-analytic procedures which combine the results of different studies. These can be said to have begun with Smith, Glass and Miller (1980). From this period until the present day, research questions have tended to move away from simply asking 'Does counselling work?' to 'What aspects work and where?'

### The early studies

One of the earliest studies was conducted on psychoanalysis by Fenichel (1930). It was a comprehensive review of ten years of the Berlin Psychoanalytic Institute and typifies the approach that many studies of the day adopted. Fenichel reported 1,955 initial client consultations, of whom 721 started therapy. When the report was published 363 clients had completed therapy, 241 had terminated prematurely and 117 were still in treatment. Of those who had completed treatment 147 were deemed 'uncured', 116 were said to have improved, 89 had very much improved and 11 were considered cured.

The design of the study was simplistic. There was no attempt to standardise the criteria for change or indeed, entry into therapy. Dropouts were not evaluated, which may have increased or decreased the success rate of the Institute. Probably the greatest design flaw of the study was the lack of any comparison with another group of similar patients who were given a different treatment or no treatment at all. This left two unanswered questions: What would have happened to these patients if they had been treated using other methods? How much of the effects which were claimed to be due to psychotherapy were simply a result of the passage of time?

Many other studies were conducted during this period, all of which had the major design fault mentioned above. There was a considerable resistance on the part of the practitioners to the idea of research, many claiming that the outcomes they were striving towards could not be measured. For a comprehensive review of these studies see Bergin (1971).

### From Eysenck to the beginning of meta-analysis

Eysenck (1952) delivered his salvo in a paper which had a profound effect on the rigour of subsequent research designs. First he reviewed the current literature for evidence of spontaneous remission. He found this in two sources: one from the percentage of patients who had been diagnosed as neurotic in US state mental hospitals and who had recovered or greatly improved. In the second he obtained similar amelioration rates for patients who were insured by an American health insurance company. He arrived at two very comparable figures; between 68 per cent and 72 per cent for the hospitals and 72 per cent of patients for the insurance company had recovered after five years with no treatment. Eysenck then went on to examine nineteen outcome studies on psychoanalytic and eclectic therapies. He divided the results into four categories:

1  Cured or much improved;
2  Improved;
3  Slightly improved;
4  Not improved, died or left treatment.

He further subdivided these categories into improved (categories 1 and 2) and not improved (categories 3 and 4). He finally arrived at the figure of 44 per cent for psychoanalysis and 64 per cent for eclectic therapies. His conclusions were: 'There appears to be an inverse correlation between recovery and psychotherapy, the more psychotherapy; the smaller the recovery rate.' He then went on to say:

> It would appear then, that when we discount the risk that the patient runs of stopping treatment altogether, his chances of improvement under psychoanalysis are approximately equal to his chances of improvement under eclectic treatment, and slightly worse than his chances under a general practitioner or custodial treatment.
>
> (Eysenck 1952)

As can be imagined his remarks provoked a plethora of protest and praise, polarising both psychologists and psychotherapists. His figures of two-thirds spontaneous remission rates are still (erroneously) quoted today.

Ironically, it is the poor designs of the studies that Eysenck reviewed that enable us to question his assertion that psychotherapy is ineffective. The data that Eysenck reviewed was so ambiguous that its interpretation was open to the bias of the reviewer. Bergin and Lambert (1978) produced a table of four possible interpretations of the psychoanalytic data that Eysenck reviewed, with results suggesting improvement in psychotherapy which ranged from 44 per cent using Eysenck's criteria and 83 per cent using Bergin's criteria.

The Eysenck argument was perhaps finally laid to rest by McNeilly and Howard (1991) using a dosage model of psychotherapeutic effectiveness which compares degree of improvement with the length of time (i.e. dose) needed. They conducted an analysis on Eysenck's original 'spontaneous remission' data. This was compared with a similar analysis that had been conducted by Howard et al. (1986) on a panel of patients who had received psychotherapy. They found that psychotherapy achieved in fifteen weeks what custodial treatment or GP treatment achieved in two years.

### Studies from 1953 to 1978

The number of studies that included some form of comparison group increased substantially after Eysenck's 1952 paper.

Rogers and Dymond (1954) is typical of some of these earlier studies. They divided clients into two groups, those who were given client-centred counselling and those who were assigned to a waiting list. Measures were taken before and after treatment for the treatment group, and before and after sixty days and then after subsequent counselling for the comparison group.

The main problem with this design was of selection bias. Clients were assigned to the waiting list if the researchers considered that they would come to no harm or unnecessary distress. This ensured that the more distressed group received counselling first and left problems of participants leaving one group faster than the other.

Arbuckle and Boy (1961) exemplify how research designs developed in the 1960s. They were interested in evaluating the efficacy of counselling in schools, in this case using 'client-centred' counselling. They used randomisation as the way of reducing the problems described in the study above. They randomly allocated thirty-six students with behavioural problems to three groups: a group that received individual counselling in the place of after-school detention, a control group who were treated normally and given detention and a laissez-faire control group who were released from detention but had no counselling. The groups were observed before 'treatment' and after treatment, using standardised measures which included self, peer and teacher evaluation. The results were impressively in favour of the counselled group. With the exception of rather small numbers, this was a well-designed study.

From this time on there was a profusion of outcome studies using a variety of designs. There is no space in this review, nor is it appropriate, to examine a large number of studies individually. Many authors have done so (e.g. Bergin 1971). Most of the studies were of behavioural or client-centred therapy, and psychoanalytic therapy was largely omitted. In order to rectify this, a central fact-gathering committee was set up by the American Psychoanalytic Society. The committee's history is a reflection of how difficult it was for psychoanalytic psychotherapists and analysts to monitor their work. The committee was dissolved in 1957, set up once more and again dissolved. It was reformed in 1961 and after six years published its results. Less than a third of those who had started psychotherapy (3,019 out of an initial 10,000) had had information kept about them before and after treatment; the rest had been lost or was simply missing. Of this highly skewed sample only 27 per cent overall showed reductions in symptoms, although 97 per cent of patients and therapists reported that they had improved. Patients who had improved tended to be highly educated and to have been in analysis, which was found to be significantly more effective than psychotherapy. The conclusion of the committee was that more moderately scaled and sharply focused measures should be used in the future. They also pleaded for more *inter rater* reliability and expressed dissatisfaction with the overall data collection process. An expensive and salutary lesson had been learnt for future psychotherapy researchers.

Bergin and Lambert (1978) summarised the studies that had been conducted between 1953 and 1969. They stated that most of the studies had aimed at establishing whether or not psychotherapy 'works', something that was shown only to a moderate degree. It would appear that the better the design the more the positive the effect measured. However there seemed to be no relationship between therapist orientation, length of treatment and outcome.

As a summary of the contemporary research, Bergin and Lambert's (1978) review was hardly a glowing endorsement for psychotherapy. In spite of this, studies after this time tended to ask research questions in classes I and II (see p. 39). The question, 'Does psychotherapy/ counselling work?' was still being asked, but tended to be embedded in more specific questions. It was not until the advent of meta-analytic techniques, developed in the late 1970s and early 1980s, that it re-emerged as a valid question and can be said to have been finally laid to rest.

*Meta-analytic studies, 1978 onwards*

An obvious difficulty of comparing different studies with each other, particularly in the field of counselling research, is their sheer diversity. This diversity extends not only to the methodology used but to the measures used, the sample number, therapist and client variables, the mode and model of therapy and length of study, to mention but a few. To exemplify this difficulty let us look at the diversity of measures used in psychotherapy research. Froyd and Lambery (1989) reviewed 348 outcome studies that were conducted over the five-year period between 1983 and 1989. They found that 1,430 outcome measures had been used, of which 840 had been used only once. Even when a second review was conducted on outcome studies that had been carried out on a specific disorder (Ogles et al. 1990), it was found that 98 different measures had been used.

Perhaps as a consequence of these difficulties, the technique or group of techniques called meta-analysis was developed. Meta-analysis can be simply defined as the application of empirical techniques to literature review. A number of studies are chosen, using predefined categories such as the use of some form of randomisation. A way of comparing the results of the studies is then established. Some form of weighting the methodologies, sample size, inclusion criteria, and so on is devised in order to standardise the studies. Statistical techniques are then used to compare the studies and establish any overall statistical significance.

Meta-analytic techniques were developed by Smith and Glass in the late 1970s (Glass 1976, 1977; Glass & Smith, 1979; Smith & Glass, 1977). It was the last of these papers that created the greatest impact and once again started academic controversies. The main results of the study were that a client who has been treated with some form of counselling is likely to be better off than 80 per cent of people who have had no treatment at all. This compares favourably with other forms of psychological, pharmacological and educational interventions. For instance, patients treated with drug therapy, for example antidepressants, were between 80 per cent and 69 per cent better off than those who were untreated, depending on the medication used and the severity of the initial problem (Lambert & Bergin 1994). Even if we take into account that the drug trial sample tended to be older and have more severe disorders, there is little to choose between the two treatments.

A number of workers conducted critical reviews of the Smith (1980) paper and arrived at very similar results. Andrews and Harvey (1981) reviewed eighty-one studies of neurotic patients and found that the percentage figure was a 76 per cent improvement over untreated patients. Landerman and Dawes (1982) analysed forty-two studies of mixed diagnosis and found that the percentage was around 82 per cent. Other reviewers included new studies in their reviews and again arrived at similar figures (Miller & Berman 1983; Dush et al. 1983).

The controversy about the efficacy of psychotherapy was not yet over. The criticisms levelled at the Smith et al. paper (1980), particularly those of Rachman and Wilson (1980), had not been entirely laid to rest. Shapiro and Shapiro (1982) conducted a meta-analysis using some of the Smith et al. data but added many other studies that had been published two years after their 1977 deadline. The Shapiros considered the criticisms of Rachman and Wilson and, although not completely agreeing with them, conducted a meta-analysis as *if* they were plausible. They reviewed 143 studies, preferring studies that compared two forms of psychotherapy and including only studies that recorded untreated or minimally treated controls. They included more behavioural studies and did not include any unpublished work such as doctoral theses. They also refined the categories used to define the outcome measures. The results that they obtained were even more in favour of psychotherapy than those of Smith and Glass (1980). Once again, significant and consistent gain had been achieved by those therapies.

It would seem that the argument as to whether psychotherapy and counselling work compared to no treatment has been put to rest. Overall, psychotherapy and counselling are more effective than the 'natural healing process'. The arguments as to whether psychotherapy is effective have had the effect of making it highly researched and validated. In fact, according to Howard et al. (1995), no other clinical intervention has had anywhere near that amount of empirical evidence to back it up. However, to state simply that psychotherapy and counselling work is like saying that antibiotics work. Exactly how they work and which aspects of them work and which do not, is not answered. With new improved therapies that are 'quite different from conventional therapies' being developed with astonishing rapidity, these questions become all the more important.

## The future of counselling research and its effect on practice

There is a growing distinction between clinical counselling and personal growth. This tends to be related to the context in which the counselling takes place and who is paying for it. Personal growth may be seen as an endeavour for which an individual pays and which is often open-ended. Clinical counselling may be paid for by another body such as an employer or GP and tends to be time sensitive. This may be related to the fact that counselling in the UK is becoming more professional. It is no longer mainly in the domain of the private practitioner and is increasingly being used in organisational settings, health settings and education. In doing so it is becoming more accountable and so more research based. Parry (1996: 41) states in the NHS report on psychological therapies: 'research findings on efficacy and clinical effectiveness of the psychotherapies are the starting point for evidence-based practice'. She then goes on to say:

> Those responsible for purchasing psychological therapies should not
> fund services or procedures where there is clear empirical evidence

that they are ineffective . . . purchasing strategy should drive forward the agenda of evidence-based practice by moving investment towards those psychology, counselling and psychotherapy services a) which have adopted clinical guidelines for standard practice b) where the guidelines are informed by the findings of research and service evaluation c) which specify the patient groups for which the service is appropriate, d) which monitor outcomes for innovative treatment e) which audit key elements of standard practice.

(Parry 1996: 47)

### The shape of things to come?

As in many areas of culture it is likely that the UK will go, some way at least, down the path taken by the USA. There, there has been an increasing trend away from the private practitioner towards group practices, which in turn have been subsumed into larger health management organisations (HMOs) (Hoyt 1995). These multi-million-dollar corporations service the mental health needs of large populations on a per capita basis. This means that they estimate the incidence of specific psychological disorders in a given population and then charge a flat fee to primary care physicians and large corporations for the provision of a complete mental health service. This includes counselling. The HMOs are financed by medical insurance companies, perhaps not renowned for their altruism. These companies want evidence of effective practice and, of course, cost effectiveness. This evidence is provided by research. Comprehensive audit and quality control is also carried out as a matter of course.

So does this mean that evidence based models of counselling such as cognitive-behavioural therapy (CBT) will come to dominate counselling, leaving their less researched relatives in the margins of private practice? Probably not. The success of CBT in being recognised by many purchasers has not gone unnoticed by researchers, and in many ways there has been a 'post-Eysenck'-like increase in research into other models of counselling. This is not without its difficulties. CBT has its roots in research and, as far as any counselling is easy to research, its goals are relatively simple to verify. However, new methods of research are being devised and there is a gradual recognition that the gold standard of research designs, the randomised controlled trial (RCT), has not travelled from its drug trail origins without some problems. Other models of working, such as short-term dynamic therapy and interpersonal therapy, are all building up a body of research literature to support their use (Robinson et al. 1990). To muddy the waters further there is a move towards working integratively and using specific evidence-based interventions for specific problems (Roth &

Fonagy 1996), meaning that practitioners using one exclusive model of working may become a practice of the past.

How, then, will research impact on practice? The internal market in the NHS is being developed with the advent of GP consortia and there is a rise in the number of employee assistance schemes whereby confidential counselling is offered to employees of organisations. Both these developments fit well into the HMO research-oriented model of service provision which may well not be far away. It could take the form of counsellors who are currently in group practices bidding for work from local GP consortia. These practices may in turn grow into larger organisations in much the same way as they did in the USA. Another possibility is that as the US 'market' becomes saturated, the large conglomerates may invest in the UK, bringing with them work practices that have been honed in a highly competitive environment. Even if these scenarios are not realised, a knowledge of research and the use of evaluation and audit is likely to take on a much higher profile in a clinical counsellor's practice.

# References

Abramowitz, C.V. & Dokecki, P.R. (1977). The politics of clinical judgement: Early empirical returns. *Psychological Bulletin*, 84, 460–476.

Andrews, G. & Harvey, R. (1981). Does psychotherapy benefit neurotic patients? A re-analysis of the Smith, Glass and Miller data. *Archives of General Psychiatry*, 38, 1203–1208.

Arbuckle, D.S. & Boy, A.V. (1961). Client-centred therapy in counselling students with behavior problems. *Journal of Counseling Psychology*, 8, 136–139.

Beck, A.T., Rush, A.J., Shaw, B.F. and Emery, G. (1979). *Cognitive Therapy of Depression*. New York: Guilford Press.

Bergin, A.E. (1971). The evaluation of therapeutic outcomes. In A.E. Bergin & S.L. Garfield (eds). *Handbook of Psychotherapy and Behavior Change* (1st Edition). New York: Wiley, 217–270.

Bergin, A.E. & Lambert, M.J. (1978). The Evaluation of Therapeutic Outcomes. In A.E. Bergin and S.L. Garfield (eds). *Handbook of Psychotherapy and Behavior Change* (2nd edition). New York: Wiley, 139–190.

Buros, O.K. (ed.) (1978). *The VIIIth Mental Measurement Yearbook*. Highland Park, NJ: Griffon Press.

Cook, T.D. & Campbell, D.T. (1979). *Quasi-experimentation: Design and Analysis Issues for Field Settings*. Boston: Houghton Mifflin.

Crits-Christoph, P., Baranackie, K., Kurcias, J.S., Beck, A.T., Carroll, K., Perry, K., Luborsky, L., McLellan, A., Woody, G.E., Thompson, L., Gallaher, D. & Zitrin, C. (1991). Meta-analysis of therapist effects in psychotherapy outcome studies. *Psychotherapy Research*, 1, 81–92.

Dawes, R.M. (1986). Representative thinking in clinical judgment. *Clinical Psychology Review*, 6, 425–441.

Dush, D.M., Hirt, M.L. & Schroder, H. (1983). Self statement modification with adults: A meta-analysis. *Journal of Consulting and Clinical Psychology*, 94, 408–422.

Eysenck, H.J. (1952). The effects of psychotherapy: An evaluation. *Journal of Consulting Psychology*, 16, 319–324.

Fenichel, O. (1930). *Ten Years of the Berlin Psychoanalytic Institute, 1920–1930*. Berlin: Berlin Psychoanalytic Institute.

Friedman, N. (1967). *The Social Nature of Psychological Research*. New York: Basic Books.

Froyd, J., & Lambery, M.J. (1989). A Survey of Outcome Research Measures in Psychotherapy Research. Paper presented at the meeting of the Western Psychological Association, Reno, NV.

Glass, G.V. (1976). Primary, secondary and meta-analysis of research. *Educational Researcher*, 5, 3–8.

Glass, G.V. & Smith, M. L. (1979). Meta analysis of research on the relationship of class-size and achievement. *Educational Evaluation and Policy Analysis*, 1, 2–16.

Hemmings, A.J. (1997). Health Service Journal, 12th–18th June.

Heppner, P.P., Kivlighan, D.M & Wampold, B.E. (1992). *Research Design in Counseling*. Pacific Grove, CA: Brooks/Cole.

Howard, K.I., Krause, M.S. & Orlinski, D.E. (1986). The attrition dilemma: Towards a new strategy for psychotherapy research. *Journal of Consulting and Clinical Psychology*, 54, 106–110.

Howard, K.I., Orlinski, D.E. & Lueger, R.L. (1995). The design of clinically relevant outcome research: Some considerations and an example. In M. Aveline and D. Shapiro (eds). *Research Foundations for Psychotherapy Practice*. Chichester: Wiley, 3–47.

Hoyt, H.F. (1995). *Brief Therapy and Managed Care: Readings for contemporary practice*. San Francisco: Jossey Bass.

Hurvitz, N. (1970). Interaction hypothesis in marriage counselling. *The Family Coordinator*. 19, 64–75.

Kazdin, A.E. (1980). *Research Design in Clinical Psychology*. New York: Harper & Row.

Kerlinger, F.N. (1986). *Foundations of Behavioral Research* (3rd edition). New York: Holt Rinehart & Wilson.

Kline, P. (1986). *The Handbook of Test Construction*. London: RKP.

Kline, P. (1993). *The Handbook of Psychological Testing*. London: RKP.

Lambert, M.J. & Bergin, A.E. (1994). The effectiveness of psychotherapy. In A.E. Bergin & S.L. Garfield (eds). *Handbook of Psychotherapy and Behavior Change* (4th edition). New York: Wiley, 143–189.

Lambert, M.J., Masters, K.S. & Ogles, B.M. (1991). Outcome research in counselling. In C.E. Watkins and L.J. Schneider (eds). *Research in Counselling*. Hillsdale, NJ: Lawrence Erlbaum Associates, 51–84.

Landerman, J.T. & Dawes, R.M. (1982). Psychotherapy outcome: Smith and Glass conclusions stand up under scrutiny. *American Psychologist*, 37, 504–516.

Lieberman, M.L., Yalom, I.D. & Miles, M.B. (1973). *Encounter groups: First facts*. New York: Basic Books.

McNeilly, C.L. & Howard, K.I. (1991). The effects of psychotherapy: A re-evaluation based on dosage. *Psychotherapy Research*, 1, 74–78.

Miller, R.C. & Berman, J.S. (1983). The efficacy of cognitive behavior therapies: A quantitative review of the research evidence. *Psychological Bulletin*, 94, 39–53.

Ogles, B.N., Lambert, M.J., Weight, D.G. and Payne, I.R. (1990). Agoraphobia outcome measurement: A review and meta-analysis. *Journal of Consulting and Clinical Psychology*, 2, 317–325.

Orlinski, D. and Howard, K.I. (1978). The relation of process to outcome in psychotherapy. In A.E. Bergin & S.L. Garfield (eds). *Handbook of Psychotherapy and Behavior Change* (2nd edition). New York: Wiley, 283–330.

Orne, M.Y. & Wender, P.H. (1968). Anticipatory socialization for psychotherapy: Method and rationale. *American Journal of Psychiatry*, 124, 1202–1212.

Parry, G. (1996). *NHS Psychotherapy Services in Review of Strategic Quality*. London: NHS Executive.

Rachman, S.J. & Wilson, G.T. (1980). *The Effects of Psychological Therapy* (2nd enlarged edition). New York: Pergamon.

Rennie, D.L. (1994). Human science and counselling psychology: Closing the gap between research and practice. A paper given at the Counselling Division of the British Psychological Society annual conference.

Robinson, L.A., Berman, J.S., & Neimeyer, R.A. (1990). Psychotherapy for the treatment of depression: A comprehensive review of controlled outcome research. *Psychological Bulletin*, 108, 30–49.

Rogers, C.R. & Dymond, R. (1954). *Psychotherapy and Personality Change*. Chicago: University of Chicago Press.

Rosenthal, R. & Rosnow, R.L. (1969). The volunteer subject. In R. Rosenthal & R.L. Rosnow (eds), *Artefact in Behavioral Research*. New York: Academic Press, 61–118.

Roth, A. & Fonagy, P. (1996) *What Works for Whom? A Critical Review of Psychotherapy Research*. New York: Guildford.

Scholes, J. & Freeman, M.A. (1994). The Reflective Dialogue and Repertory Grids: A method for examining the therapeutic milieu of health visitors and midwives. *The Journal of Advanced Nursing*, 20, 885–893.

Shapiro, D.A., Barkham, M., Rees, A., Hardy, G.E., Reynolds, S. & Startup, M. (1994). Effects of treatment duration and severity of depression on the effectiveness of cognitive/behavioural and psychodynamic/interpersonal psychotherapy. *Journal of Consulting and Clinical Psychology*, 62, 522–534.

Shapiro, D.A. & Shapiro, D. (1982). Meta-analysis of comparative therapy outcome studies: A replication and refinement. *Psychological Bulletin*, 92, 581–604.

Shaw, M.L.G. (1993). *Manual to RepGrid 2 programme*. Calgary: Centre for person computer studies.

Sloane, R.B., Staples, F.R., Cristol, A.H., Yorkston, N.J. & Whipple, K. (1975). *Psychotherapy Versus Behavior Therapy*. Cambridge, Mass.: Harvard University Press.

Smith, M.L. & Glass, G.V. (1977). Meta-analysis of psychotherapy outcome studies. *American Psychologist*, 32, 752–760.

Smith, M.L., Glass, G.V. & Miller, T.I. (1980). *The Benefits of Psychotherapy.* Baltimore: Johns Hopkins University Press.

Storr, A. (1983). *The Art of Psychotherapy.* London: Secker & Warburg.

Strupp, H.H. & Hadley, S.W. (1977). A tripartite model of mental health and therapeutic outcome. With special reference to negative effects in psychotherapy. *American Psychologist, 32,* 187–196.

Tversky, A., & Kahnerman, D. (1974). Judgment under uncertainty: Heuristics and biases. *Science, 185,* 1124–1131.

# 4  Time-limited work in context

*June Roberts*

In this chapter I place psychodynamic counselling within the socio-historical context of the development of the helping professions in Britain. I will then look at time-limited counselling from the point of view of three questions:

- Are brief therapeutic interventions simply a convenient way of dealing with the economic restrictions on therapeutic work, or do they have value in their own right?
- When is time-limited work desirable and when is long-term work desirable?
- Is time-limited work based on a superficial theory or is it a sophisticated agent of therapeutic change?

I will illustrate the first of these questions with a case study, in order to demonstrate how a time-limited intervention may provoke a positive focus on developmental conflict, thus assisting in its resolution. Another example is offered in relation to the second question, before I move on to the third question and a discussion of brief dynamic therapy and counselling, which highlights their powerful potential in the hands of practitioners whose own therapeutic needs have been adequately met.

> One way of mishandling a problem is to behave as if it did not exist. For this form of denial we have borrowed the term 'terrible simplification'. Two consequences follow from it: a) acknowledgment, let alone any attempted solution, of the problem is seen as a manifestation of madness or badness; and b) the problem requiring change becomes greatly compounded by the 'problems' created through its mishandling.
>
> (Watzlawick et al. 1974: 46)

## Background

Entering social work in the 1960s as a total greenhorn, I blundered into the debate, characterized in those days as psychodynamic casework versus material aid, which included practical problem-solving and the provision of things like blankets or a new roof. It was Barbara Wootton, of social policy fame, who sharply satirized the theorizing derived from psychoanalysis that was current in social work training and in the child-guidance clinics of the day. Some casework was brief but most was extended, whilst material aid, as ever, was subject to strict budgetary control. Alongside this kind of social provision, incarceration of delinquents, criminals and the mentally ill was running at a high level, together with the 'warehousing' of the elderly in large residential homes. Sociologists the while were writing about deviancy amplification, labelling and the relative merits of radical non-intervention. As I remember it, personnel in the core professions were heavily imbued with the idealism of the left, commitment to the welfare state and to the alleviation of poverty and social disadvantage. Jobs were freely available and most social agencies enjoyed an encouraging degree of solvency.

However, economic and structural change in the 1970s and 1980s soon put paid to all this, or at least to the part of it which was seen as doing nothing in a psychodynamic way, as the gradual demise of preventive casework and the severe restriction of material resources reduced social service departments and eroded their earlier idealism. By this time, however, a not inconsiderable pathway to social mobility had opened up, as courses strove to recruit a wider range of applicants to the profession. Class was no longer a restricting factor and discrimination against ethnic minorities was reduced, resulting in an increasing volume of eager entrants of all ages. For many of them it was the legacy of the welfare state ideology which imbued their chosen career with the possiblity of practical idealism and fulfilment, as well as a reasonable level of financial reward and security.

At the end of the 1990s the trend is quite different: medicine, teaching and social work all find it hard to retain staff while many potential entrants find greater esteem and remuneration in business, the law and financial services. Those who are more strongly drawn towards the interpersonal field and the alleviation of distress choose counselling, psychotherapy or even management consultancy as the means. The powerful dialectic which gave us so much energy in the 1960s and early 1970s has given way, dare I suggest, to an avoidance of social reality which is all too easily espoused in the confines of the consulting room. Here we may practise, with our colours nailed firmly to the mast of theoretical authenticity, the dogma of 'skills', the need for an income or a combination of all three. Daily the number of practitioners, qualified and unqualified, increases, and with them the openings for counselling and therapy which are the subject matter of this book. Simultaneously, we have seen the growth in acceptability of counselling in its peculiarly British forms, which, like social work specialisms, are often linked to particular problems, conditions or situations.

Since I became involved with time-limited therapeutic counselling interventions I have been the fortunate recipient of invitations to counselling centres and clinics between Nottingham and Totnes, to meet with bands of enthusiasts putting in hours to train, sometimes for insignificant pay, so that they may engage in the magic of the therapeutic encounter. Employee assistance programmes and occupational health departments are spreading their networks countrywide, and bit by bit GPs in rural and urban districts alike are becoming converted to the need for counselling. When we consider the demand for counselling I think it may be seen that it is created not only by the clients and potential clients but by the practitioners and providers themselves. Training has certainly become a relatively big and competitive business. Hence counselling is reaching the parts which orthodox psychotherapy never did, and the contentious clinical conundrum of short versus long, time-limited versus open-ended is brought to the centre of the stage by the logistics, financial and otherwise, of the various settings which it occupies. There may or may not be complementary motivation between client and counsellor as the working agreement is negotiated; a common need to make the contract work for the individual, for the practitioner and perhaps for the provider, who also has a stake, either latent or overt, in the outcome of the work.

I will now examine time-limited psychodynamic counselling from the point of view of the three questions that I posed earlier:

- Are brief therapeutic interventions simply a convenient way of dealing with the economic restrictions on therapeutic work, or do they have value in their own right?
- When is time-limited work desirable and when is long-term work desirable?
- Is time-limited work based on a superficial theory or is it a sophisticated agent of therapeutic change?

## Treatment of choice or convenience?

In the case of the first question, Molnos (1995: 9–12) has documented the many forms of resistance within the world of psychotherapy to the very idea of brief interventions, and adds that 'the therapist's status remains safe as long as she agrees with the general opinion that it would be so much better to do long-term work "if only we had the resources"'; the first assumption being that this is self-evident and the second that the client would be bound to agree. Working in a time-limited team at WPF Counselling, I very occasionally have the opportunity to sit with clients as they consider their options on re-entering counselling. It is an education to hear them balancing the needs of the unconscious against their well-perceived wish to resolve a recurring conflict, be it internal or external in its manifestations. This I juxtapose with the frequent assertions by psychotherapist colleagues that the client cannot know how long their treatment should last. What I think we can know is that the planned ending of a therapeutic contract is less anxiety-provoking than the uncertainty of not knowing, or of expecting a review. 'The prolongation of treatment always serves the neurosis' (Alexander & French 1974).

The other 'given' in the situation is that longer therapies use more resources than shorter ones, and longer waiting lists cause more disturbance than shorter ones. Choice, where duration of therapeutic work is concerned, is therefore contingent upon a number of variables outside the actual therapeutic alliance. Correspondingly, there are constraints in place when we approach the question 'Does brief therapy have a value in its own right?' I will not presume to attempt an answer in this chapter; rather I will invite the reader to consider the following example as some kind of paradigm.

For the purpose of anonymity the client will be called Joseph. He comes from an Eastern European country and he is a survivor of the Holocaust. He arrives at the agency by referral from a well-known forensic clinic, from where his analyst of nearly twenty years had recently retired. Joseph is in his middle fifties and is married to a woman who is some fifteen years his junior. Whilst he is clearly still mourning the analyst, he expresses an urgent need for further therapy and only reluctantly accepts a time-limited agreement. He bonds with me, to all intents and purposes like a twelve-year-old who finds himself without other means of support. The presenting issue is his criminality, which he assumes will interest and engage me as it had done those at the previous clinic. He is a fraudster and a thief of long standing. I decline to accept this focus, deferring to the failure of the analytical work to which he seemed to have clung like a limpet. He is a clever man with legal and financial expertise, and has worked for a considerable number of years as a company secretary. When I ask what else we might work on together he expresses the hope that he can rehabilitate himself in society through voluntary work and through regaining a position of trust in the world of work. He was amazed that after a successful period of prison visiting he was stopped in his tracks when the authorities traced his convictions, having discovered that he was using an alias. I felt that I could support him in this wish, even though the process of achieving it might be tortuous. I was aware that such an outcome would involve a reworking of his central conflict, but I was not entirely clear what form that might take.

During the work he repeatedly confronted me with his delinquency, shoplifting on the way to the session and carrying a briefcase that seemed menacingly likely to contain illicit material. I suppose that I punished him fairly and without malice by holding to our contract and dealing gently with his protestations. My sense was that we reworked his adolescence: I was his good object while he cast his wife in the role of the depriver. (Later I was to learn that their marriage was very much alive.) As we approached the end of our sessions he pleaded to be allowed to stay and expressed the conviction that his criminal activities would have to cease. At this point he was not cured and begged for a referral for cognitive-behavioural therapy. I suggested that he see how things went before plunging into a new endeavour. Three months later he wrote to me, using an old stamp thinly disguised, and asked to come for a follow-up session. This was a surprisingly happy reunion, but Joseph had brought me the details of his local hospital so that I could refer him to the clinical psychology department.

Apparently he was offered an appointment some weeks later but the psychologist sent him away with a flea in his ear, telling him to 'sew up his pockets!' He wrote to me again demanding another referral. I sent him an extremely explicit letter of referral to the Maudsley Hospital, and in due time they assessed him thoroughly and expertly, as I would have expected. They agreed to try to effect the cure which had seemed unrealistic to me on the basis of my assessment six months earlier. Unfortunately for Joseph, the painstaking work which ensued came too late to pre-empt a prosecution by the Department of Health and Social Security for fraud which he had perpetrated on them for a period of years prior to his work with me. Breaking the generally accepted therapeutic boundaries I agreed to appear as an expert witness, since the Maudsley would only send a long and extremely complex written report.

What became apparent during this proceeding was that Joseph was through his adolescent obduracy and ready to look at his very deep losses in their reality, rather than as a mere rejection by the father who sent him to safety. He was honest with the court and brought a large number of previous offences to be taken into consideration. He was given a sub-stantial number of hours of community service and a fine, to the chagrin of the barrister for the Crown, who argued for a long prison sentence. Subsequently he resumed contact with the Jewish community that he had ignored throughout his life in England, and made a visit to his country of origin. I believe his grieving was synonymous, or at least simultaneous, with his rehabilitation. This, of course, was his own chosen outcome to the many years of his therapy. Referring to my own work with Joseph, I believe that time-limited therapy was desirable in this case, even though the client would have chosen to work open-endedly.

## When is time-limited work desirable?

In order to give further consideration to the second question, I am going to offer another client's experience as an illustration of the clinical dilemmas and opportunities which may arise in the context of the serious developmental deficits that many people sustain.

Martin grew up in Middle England, his mother having given up a university education on her marriage to a man who later had a successful professional career. Martin's parents divorced and his father remarried while Martin was at boarding school. He was the third son of the family, the first two being twins. All were maternally deprived but Martin in particular appeared from an early age to shoulder the very real burden of looking after his mother. His whole demeanour is one of responsibility and care. He is talented and artistic, but wasn't able to benefit much from an education during which he was quite often bullied or exploited for his palpable goodwill. On leaving school he attempted to adopt a conventional lifestyle and to engage in respectable and boring jobs. This was a great failure, and he began to feel that his life lacked structure and purpose other than to continue as a handyman and cleaner for the mother, who seemed to see him as little more than a chattel.

This, together with the loss of one of his brothers in a motorcycle accident, combined to send him completely off the rails and cause what sounds like a psychotic episode followed by hospitalization and a diagnosis, while still in his early twenties, of manic depression. Heavy medication was the treatment prescribed. In the early stages of his breakdown in his usual level of his functioning, Martin did seek help. Unfortunately, this was of an evangelical nature and actually exacerbated his already overbearing conscience, effectively making him feel worse. Arguably the opportunity to engage in a responsible dynamic therapy or counselling at this stage might have prevented Martin from attracting such a heavy-duty diagnosis and becoming a fully paid-up psychiatric patient. When he came to the agency in which I was working he was in his thirties and learning a trade. His fear was that the domestic demands of the wife he had met during his most vulnerable period would cause him to lose control and become violent, a prospect which was all too familiar to his psyche. At assessment he was not seen as suitable for long-term counselling, partly because, in view of his diagnosis, he would then have had to wait for some months until a vacancy arose with a staff member, rather than a trainee. On these slightly expedient grounds he was sent to the time-limited team. Since he had caused some alarm with his threats of violence, and declined a consultation with his wife, I took him into an immediate vacancy and learned a great deal from him.

He found the planned time limit of four months encouraging and containing. He wanted to make sense of his experiences as a patient, to become more calm at home and, clearly, to enjoy some positive attention and regard. We set about working on these with the benefit of an immediate warm alliance. Because I was something of a novice in the time-limited approach at that time we were nearly halfway through the sessions before I was able to take a firm hold on my counter-transference – I actively enjoyed the attention he was used to giving his mother, but the acknowledgment of this was to bring an important development in the work. Martin became able to assert himself more with his wife, in a much calmer way. They improved the division of labour in the flat, and he was able to claim more peace and quiet for himself. With my support he relived the wild episode of his young adulthood by recalling his feelings without rejecting them. He began to understand his 'mad' phase as having some sense to it, and also to acknowledge that he had feelings of his own about his brother's sudden death, which were quite separate from those of his mother. He discussed the possibility of asking for reassessment at the psychiatric out-patients' clinic, so that he would not need to be continuously medicated for his mania. I recall a quotation which he linked to the breakdown which was the culmination of his childhood experiences: 'Each outcry of the hunted hare, a fibre from the brain' (William Blake).

In the light of this reference to the fraying of his natural abilities I was rather pleased when he returned to the agency four years later, apparently under pressure from the decision to re-enter education to take a degree. Being an experienced client/patient he asked for reassessment, fearing that any other request might not be well received. I was asked to see him and was able to spend an hour and a half encouraging him to tell me what had brought him back and hearing how he was generally pleased with his life; the only drawback being the tendency of his mother to make continuing demands, and to fail to acknowledge Martin's wife as a member of the family. An interesting development occurred when he prepared for the end of the session in under the hour. This was because of my lamentable failure to specify the time available at the beginning of the session. The subject that I had raised at this point was that of his medication. It proved to be a most effective catalyst, bringing forth a surprising amount of rather shamefaced admission by Martin – this despite his very conscientious manoeuvres designed to try to maintain his stability. What he had decided after his sessions with me were at an end was that he would try to maintain himself without dependency on a particular invididual. The GP with whom he had quite an intense relationship was on leave of absence and he was reluctant to go back to the psychiatric clinic where he had been a patient. Instead he managed to arrange lithium prescriptions (a low dose, he thought) and blood tests, for monitoring purposes. In a sense he saw himself as self-managing, but he also showed regret for having to live with the edge taken off him and with a foreign substance, of which he was aware, creating a heaviness that he would have really preferred to be without. After a bit he laughed and explained that sometimes he worked so hard doing heavy lifting and moving that he actually sweated the lithium out of his system. This made him feel good and more himself. He thought he would need the medication when he was studying. I raised the question of how long he would like to be in counselling this time, indicating that perhaps he was looking to work on an open-ended basis. He demurred and said that that was not what he intended. I suggested the possibility of meeting for six sessions and he readily agreed. Space does not allow for a detailed account of these sessions, but the material he brought was about his relationships with women and the difficulty he experienced in asserting his independence. At the end he expressed himself as well satisfied with our work, better able to resist his mother's unwelcome demands and glad that he was now making a name for himself in the work which he enjoyed. He decided to defer his place at university for a year in order to be in a better position financially, thus making more time for studying.

Here it seems important to offer the observation that clients are usually wise in their own affairs; Martin may have put his own personal development on hold, that is to say he may fear the consequences of claiming his full independence. He is attached to his wife and his home, his energy is mainly expended on physical labour. The prospect of becoming a student might hold out the promise of having some of his lost youth back, together with a rather more flexible lifestyle!

## Is time-limited work a sophisticated agent of therapeutic change?

This is the very question that is most likely to arise in a time when enterprise and the business culture is so much to the fore. Even clergy persons are now working to contracts and managing the small or large parish budget at their disposal. James Paul Gustafson wrote in *The Complex Secret of Brief Psychotherapy*:

I believe the field of psychotherapy would be much more convivial and profound if most of us were to undergo the great labour of getting a liberal education in our own field, which, I say, is a matter of putting it together for ourselves. We have had few teachers to help us towards such an aim.

(1986: 344)

The question which I prefer to put to myself, to my colleagues, and particularly to the incoming generation of counsellors and therapists, is 'What are the constituent parts of an effective therapeutic enterprise and which of these are variable, which not?' By engaging constructively in the specified time frames which our clients and sponsors present, we become able progressively to test the opposing currents within our field. An open-minded practitioner can learn significantly from clients who elect to work in fewer sessions, and which of us can honestly say that we have not had the scales removed from or eyes when working towards a planned ending?

Begging the question for a moment, and assuming that time-limited work *is* a sophisticated agent of therapeutic change, what are the constituent elements involved? On the client's side we may look for motivation, for readiness, and perhaps for some kind of developmental configuration with which we can involve ourselves purposively. The contra-indications, which are hard to transcend, include the absence of basic trust and multiple moves and separations in childhood. On the counsellor's side there is a necessity to bracket all preconceptions and assumptions, whilst looking kindly on our own defences. In other words, the progress of our own therapy may bear directly on our effectiveness when working to time limits or open-endedly. What is also important is that the counter-transference be welcome at all times in supervision. It, above all things, may be the agent of therapeutic change. Similarly, the time-limited counsellor should be calm, if not comfortable, when dealing with frame issues; both parties to the agreement will have to forge their alliance within the relative complexity of an organizational contract, a secondary setting, a lack of time for assessment and sometimes a referral by a third party whose motives may be less than disinterested. In the light of these basic considerations the widespread expediency which leads to beginners in counselling, and sometimes in psychotherapy, finding themselves in settings where only so many sessions may be offered, falls very short of being professionally desirable. A mitigating factor can arise where the agency or practice is able to provide a supervisor who is trained and experienced in time-limited work, and who enjoys facilitating new entrants. The countervailing tendency whereby 'heartsink' referrals gravitate to newcomers, who may not even be able to obtain appropriate consultation at the right time, brings us all into disrepute.

One of the surprises which may delight the newcomer to time-limited therapy and counselling is that the secrets contained in the brief dynamic approach have been discovered, affirmed, rediscovered and reconfirmed by single practitioners and groups working in clinics and centres over many decades. Ever since Alexander and French (1974) alerted their colleagues to the fact that the majority of patients did not stay in psychoanalysis for long periods and Balint in this country developed 'focal therapy' in the 1950s, therapists and counsellors, as well as social workers and clinical psychologists, have taken the leap of faith, for that is what is, of trusting the client to complete something of significance to them within a time-limited period that was brief rather than extended. What each successive team may see as an undesirable risk, carrying disapproval from clinicians and patients alike, will, in the right conditions, soon become 'a treatment of choice' for at least a proportion of clients who seek help, particularly those who are younger and those whose working lives are very pressured.

A key figure, as I see it, who spanned the middle period of the development of brief dynamic therapy and coined the term 'time-limited psychotherapy' was James Mann. Writing in 1973 he explained the secret and the rationale in this way:

> If we undertake psychotherapy of limited duration, it would be wise to begin where the patient is; namely, as soon as he learns that the amount of time for help is limited he is actively subject to the magical, timeless, omnipotent fantasies of childhood, and his expectations in respect to treatment arise from them as he lives now.
>
> (1973)

He it was who named the central conflict (unique to each client) otherwise known as the maladaptive pattern, the focus, or the core conflictual theme; in other words the heart of the matter! Molnos (1995) put it well when she said that the essential component in a successful therapy is the client's experience of their true feelings in the here and now, their feelings about the past and the recognition of the link between the two, together with a full realization of how it was that they needed to defend themself against these feelings. In the light of these clear and reasonably simple dynamic formulations, how may we understand the fact that relatively few counsellors, and proportionately even fewer supervisors, have espoused time-limited therapy or counselling as a chosen way of working?

First, as has already been indicated, the most significant element in our socialization into the profession is our own personal therapy or counselling.

In the majority of cases this will be open-ended, but where it is restricted to an arbitrary period defined by the course, or limited by finance, it may be experienced as expedient rather than therapeutic. Second, practitioners may build up preconceptions and assumptions based on a classroom introduction to psychopathology or to psychiatric classifications, rather than learning from face-to-face encounters with people. Third, we must acknowledge that we are human too; our own psychological baggage, sensitivities and wounds may cause us to shrink from time-conscious involvement with our clients' emotional conflicts. Why? Because we also know the pains of separation and loss; we too may still feel the need to defend our psyches from the unique cathartic experience which might lead us into radical change, or the continuous state of becoming which may be understood as existential awareness. Or, as Arieti put it:

> The patient has reached a critical point at which a re-alignment of psychodynamic forces and a new pattern of interpersonal relationships are due, but she is not able to muster them. This is her predicament. She is helpless. She either cannot visualise alternative cognitive structures that lead to recuperative steps or, if she is able to visualise them, they appear unsurmountable. At other times these alternatives do not seem unrealisable but worthless, since she has learned to invest all her interest and desires only in the relationship that failed.
>
> (1972: 2)

## Conclusion

This sense of investing all in a failing relationship is quite frequently a precipitating factor which prompts people to seek help, at which point a positive result may well seem more important than long-term therapy or counselling. The consequent need to do something about a painful state of affairs, and the increased accessibility of counselling, means that practitioners are under considerable pressure to address the issues raised by our three questions, to which I now return. The first draws our attention to the inherent tension between financial expediency and clinical integrity. Professionally, most of us were socialized into the open-ended culture of an essentially middle-class, fee-based activity *before* we were asked consciously to initiate, or to accept, the constraints of a time limit to our work. Often this was confused by the fact that the placements in which many trainees engage are themselves finite. The writer has often supervised counsellors who, for example, have allowed the work with clients to develop very therapeutically without ever having established the time frame in which the student is operating at the institution in which they are studying. This willingness to engage in the timelessness of a good working alliance is, of course, vital, even though it is often unrealistic and may lead to an incomplete resolution of the most significant issues in the client's life. As counsellors and therapists we need everything that open-ended practice has taught us, but this is not to say that more is better. Rather, we need the capability to sit with each and every client and calmly to consider their proposal, if there is one, our assessment and the desired outcome of the work. In the case of Joseph, with hindsight he desperately needed to resolve his adolescent conflicts and to overcome the rejection he had felt when his father sent him to England. A further open-ended contract could not, in my opinion, have helped him to do this. The point at issue may connect more to the manner and style of this negotiation than to the financial pros and cons of the situation. Where financial expediency all too often creeps in is where the profit motive of the provider is at odds with the professional judgement of the practitioner. In this situation the number of sessions dictated by the contract may not coincide with the needs of the client.

The second question, of when time-limited counselling is desirable and when open-ended, is one with which we are all confronted, I would argue, each time we meet a potential client for a first session. In Martin's case, had he met with a counsellor or therapist at the time of his first manic breakdown he would have been very likely to have benefited from a long-term therapy with psychiatric back-up, but not necessarily with medication for life. Here the reader may very possibly point out that many brief dynamic therapists would rule him out on the grounds that he was not in touch with reality. This, of course, is a matter of fine clinical judgement, not only of the mental state of the client but also of the competence of the practitioner to hold a very disturbed young adult at such a critical stage in his psychical development. By the time he reached me, in his thirties, he was fearful of the possibility of regression and felt that he could manage better in the context of a time-limited agreement. How wise he was, and how fortunate that I had institutional backing for working with him in this way! The issues involved in these decisions are clinically highly sensitive; ideally the financial arrangements would be in support, for only thus can the much more expensive possibility of further breakdown be pre-empted. Perhaps the greatest call on our sophistication lies in the experience needed to decide when to trust the client's inner wisdom and when to use our own, to initiate and maintain a time-limited working agreement.

# References

Alexander, F. and French, T.M. (1974) *Psychoanalytical Therapy: Principles and Applications*. Lincoln, NA: University of Nebraska Press.

Arieti, S. (1972) *The Will to Be Human*. New York: Quadrangle Books.

Gustafson, J.P. (1986) *The Complex Secret of Brief Psychotherapy*. New York: W.W. Norton.

Mann, J. (1973) *Time-Limited Psychotherapy*. Cambridge, MA: Harvard University Press.

Molnos, A. (1995) *A Question of Time: Essentials of Brief Dynamic Psychotherapy*. London: Karnac Books.

Watzlawick, P., Weakland, J. and Fisch, R. (1974) *Change: Principles of Problem Formation and Problem Resolution*. New York: W.W. Norton.

# 5 The problem-solving pilgrim

## A goal-orientated approach to clinical counselling

*Michael Scott*

In Chaucer's *Canterbury Tales* (Chaucer 1985) pilgrims en route to pay homage at the tomb of St Thomas à Becket in Canterbury pass the evening together, each telling a tale, often scoring points off each other, some tales much bawdier than others, reflecting their diverse backgrounds. It occurred to me after attending a conference at the University of Kent at Canterbury in the summer of 1997 and visiting Canterbury Cathedral that those pilgrims were much like modern-day counsellors. There is an underlying reverence for the client, the different counsellors tell different tales, each thinking their own is best; nevertheless there is a common purpose – to relieve if possible or sometimes just to share the emotional pain of others. The 'why?' of this endeavour is, I think, as mysterious as paying homage at the tomb. Historically, counsellors tend to have fallen into two main opposing camps: there have been cognitive-behaviourists, emphasising the technical aspects of their craft such as problem solving, and there has been the humanistic tradition, emphasising the overriding importance of the counsellor remembering their humanity. What I want to suggest is that these two traditions are not fundamentally incompatible, and that neither can function without the other – indeed that they are different ways of tackling the same phenomenon, each more appropriate in some circumstances than in others. To illustrate this latter point I will tell a 'tale' about light. For many years physicists believed that light travels in straight lines (corpuscular theory). This proved a very fruitful idea and made it possible to understand, say, how a periscope works. Then in the early part of this century came the discovery that light can bend. For example, if you put a tiny hole in a card and shine the light through you do not get a straight beam: it spreads out slightly on the other side, which suggests that light is sometimes like a wave. If you ask a physicist which is true, corpuscular theory or wave theory, the retort is traditionally 'On Monday, Wednesday and Friday light travels in straight lines but on Tuesday, Thursday and Saturday it is a wave and on Sunday even God had a day off.' The point the physicist is making is that one is no more true than the other, but one is more efficient in some circumstances than others. Thus the physicist would consistently apply, say, wave theory in one context and equally consistently apply corpuscular theory in another context. In a similar way the context of a counselling session might change within the session, so that at one period the counsellor might be teaching the client to problem solve systematically and at another period might be empathising with the client's sheer frustration. Counsellors from different theoretical orientations may look to be doing the same thing in a session, for example empathising with a client, and there is therefore often a de facto technical eclecticism, but their rationales are different and both they and their clients will become confused if counsellors are not consistent with their theoretical base.

It is fairly obvious that medieval pilgrims would have had to ensure their physical safety, protecting themselves against brigands in order to reach their holy place. Strangely, counsellors can be so focused on their interactions with the client that they do not read the context in which they are operating and run a grave risk of having their 'pilgrimage' sabotaged. This chapter therefore begins with the problem-solving pilgrim's guide to survival. The following five problem-solving operations are then outlined: (1) problem orientation; (2) problem definition and formulation; (3) generation of alternatives; (4) decision making and (5) solution implementation and verification. One way of visualising the problem-solving process is to see problem orientation as being at the top of an hourglass. This is followed by a narrowing down of the problem, until at the neck of the hourglass is the precise definition of the problem. Part of the way down the base of the hourglass is the generation of a range of alternative solutions, then further down is the choice of solutions. There then follows the implementation of solutions. Finally, at the base of the hourglass there is a review of how the solutions have worked out. If the chosen solution is ineffective the hourglass is tipped upside down and the problem-solving process begun again, leading to experimentation with another option.

## The problem-solving pilgrim's guide to survival in organisations

### The need for evidence

In Britain the National Health Service is the largest employer of counsellors and psychologists and this section is largely devoted to survival within it, but much of it can also be applied to counsellors working in other settings such as charities. Over the past decade there has been an emphasis on evidence-based medicine, that is, that clinicians should only use treatments that have demonstrated their worth in controlled trials. A journal, *Evidence Based Medicine* is devoted entirely to reviewing the results of controlled trials and commenting on their implications, and a companion journal *Evidence Based Mental Health* (British Medical Journal Publishing Group) began publication in 1998. For good or ill there is a climate change for mental health professionals and audit will be the rule of the day. In this connection Roth and Fonagy (1996) have provided a useful critical review of controlled trials of psychological interventions and outlined what works for whom. To fare well in audit the counsellor has not only to utilise strategies of demonstrated efficacy but also to choose those that can be delivered in a cost-effective way and are most acceptable to clients. This may, for example, mean running group programmes in tandem with individual programmes where possible, or choosing interventions that have a simple rationale to ensure wider acceptability. The counsellor's survival will depend on using strategies that are not only effective but also have clinical utility (see Scott & Stradling 1998).

## Ways of demonstrating efficacy

One instrument of particular use in conducting an audit in primary care is the Hospital Anxiety and Depression Scale (HAD) (Snaith & Zigmond 1983) to document the severity of patients' anxiety and depression. Anxiety and depression constitute the bulk of referrals to counsellors in primary care, with usually twice as many cases of anxiety as depression. The anxiety category consists largely of patients with either generalised anxiety disorder or panic disorder with or without agoraphobic avoidance. Other anxiety disorders such as social phobia, obsessive compulsive disorder and post-traumatic stress disorder (PTSD) are less commonly referred. An essential part of audit is to determine the various categories of patients referred: thus the counsellor should be aware of the diagnostic criteria for the various anxiety and depression disorders. The HAD (Snaith & Zigmond 1983) acts as a useful marker of the severity of anxiety or depression symptoms and progress in the resolution of those difficulties.

At a minimum the HAD ought to be administered at the initial assessment and again after five or six sessions in order to determine whether any change has occurred in the client. However, some clients are lost to audit with this method because they default after fewer than the five or six sessions. One way around this is to ask all patients to bring to a session a completed HAD. Thus the counsellor would have data on at least the last point of contact with the patient; this would then enable the counsellor to determine whether the client was defaulting because they considered themselves better (a low HAD score) or because they were still debilitated but not finding the interventions useful. The HAD ought to be administered at least every five or six sessions to monitor progress, and certainly with patients who have personality disorders it may be not until ten or fifteen sessions that there is a marked change in anxiety or depression symptoms. There are fourteen items on the HAD: seven relate to anxiety and seven to depression, with a maximum possible score of 21 on each subscale. The scale has three zones on each subscale: 0–7 is normal, 8–10 is borderline and over 10 pathological. It is thus possible to see not only the effect on a particular client but the overall pattern of results that emerge from a counsellor's practice.

There are, of course, more specific measures that relate to particular disorders, for example the PENN inventory (Hammarberg 1992) measures the severity of post-traumatic stress disorder and in a case of PTSD (which is a specific anxiety disorder) this would also be used as well as the HAD. Such an instrument furnishes additional information that would be useful to the counsellor. For example, one of the items on the PENN concerns the client indicating that there are aspects of their trauma that they have said almost nothing about to anybody. Clearly, this would be a focal concern of the counsellor. However, no matter what the disorder, improvement would be reflected in a change on the HAD scale. The audit also allows the counsellor to see how many patients with different disorders are being referred to them and to consider whether there would be sufficient numbers in any one category to run a group programme as a component of treatment. Individual and group therapy should not be seen as diametrically opposed: clients with a particular condition have sufficient in common that a group educational component can be legitimated. However, for most conditions there are likely to be sufficient features that are idiosyncratic and highly personal to justify supplementary individual sessions. The effect of running a group module is to save time, and there can also be clinical benefits as patients can see the ways in which other individuals are disturbing themselves and become better able to deal with their own distress in trying to resolve the distress of others. Other members of the group can model effective coping. At a practical level, however, it can be difficult in any one practice to get sufficient numbers of patients with a disorder at any one time to run a group and a waiting list may need to be developed. The author's experience is that in a group practice of eight thousand patients and four or five referring GPs it is possible to have sufficient referrals of patients with generalised anxiety disorder to form a group and probably, but less frequently, groups for patients with panic disorder and depression. The author's experience is that it is unwise to mix groups of both anxious and depressed patients, as the depressive patients tend to become irritated that they do not make progress as rapidly as the anxiety sufferers.

### Surviving organisational dynamics

Counsellors, almost by definition, have to believe in the potential of a client to grow or develop skills and it is then but a short step to believe that organisations such as the NHS and charities that have clients as their focal point are amenable to redemption. It is easy to forget that an organisation is not a single moral individual and is therefore not likely to behave as one. In looking at the dynamics of your particular organisational setup and its mission statements the counsellor is living dangerously if they forget that organisations are inherently exploitative, in that the more a person does the more will be asked of them. Organisations usually work hard at getting people addicted to them, implying that there is no life beyond the organisation. It is for the individual counsellor to assess their limited amount of energy and decide on what is the most efficient use of that energy, hopefully to enjoy working for the organisation but not be addicted to it. In some instances the organisation is toxic and the counsellor may have to mentally distance from it and, like an undercover policeman, carry on their good work with the client as best they can. Like the pilgrim of old, the counsellor has a higher goal to pursue, but in may instances to vocalise this to the organisation would be to 'cast pearls before swine'.

## Problem orientation

Problem orientation refers to 'locking' on to problems. This, in the author's experience, is often the most difficult stage of problem solving. Clients deficient in problem-orientation skills do not see their distress consisting of a series of discrete problems, but rather describe their difficulties in an over-generalised way, for example 'it's awful', 'it's not fair', and so on. They usually have the intellectual power to resolve the difficulty, in the sense that if they were given the problem in an examination or if a friend presented them with the particular problem domain they could come up with solutions and resolve it. Problem-orientation difficulties can be likened to someone using a spanner: they have the strength to turn a nut but they have difficulty in getting the spanner on to the nut in the first place.

The counsellor's role can be conceptualised as helping the client to close the gap between their current state and some desired state (i.e to problem solve) but if in effect the client believes the desired state is impossible, then the counsellor faces an impossible task. This scenario can present in various ways. Recently the author had referred to him by a GP a patient who had many years ago suffered 50 per cent burns. He had a score of 18 on the anxiety subscale of the HAD and 14 on the depression subscale, so he was severely anxious and moderately depressed. Almost his opening sentence when I saw him was that he had come because his wife thought he needed to and that he needed to sort out his irritable outbursts. However, it soon transpired that he believed his depression, anxiety and irritability were the only legitimate response to the death of family members years earlier in the fire and his embarrassment about his scarring. The GP was very concerned because he had had three overdoses, all at Christmas time, in the previous three years. He was not orientated to changing his view about himself, though he could contemplate a goal of moving from his present state of irritability with his children to a state where he had fewer outbursts. Thus he was only problem orientated to a very limited extent.

In some instances clients simply wish to tell the counsellor how awful their life is and they use the sessions simply for this purpose. This tends to produce only momentary relief for the client and leaves the fundamental problems unresolved. One way of tackling this 'dumping', if the counsellor has developed sufficient rapport with the client, is to perform a role reversal and have a client sit in the counsellor's chair and mimic the start of the session. This usually results in laughter from the client and the point is then made that continuing to 'awfulise' about matters is not going to get anywhere. Not only is it necessary for the client to be problem orientated, the counsellor must also be problem orientated in the sense that they must have a clear idea which emotional disorder the client has and be utilising diagnostic criteria in this process. Just as the development and evaluation of effective medications for disorders such as schizophrenia and depression has required clear criteria for these disorders, so the counsellor must know clearly what ails the client in order to proffer appropriate help. An important part of the orientation process is for the counsellor to narrate to the client a 'tale' of their particular disorder. This can be done both verbally and graphically. The following are the 'tales' told by the author to clients with depression, panic disorder and generalised anxiety disorder:

*Depression*

Depression is like blowing a fuse, you've gone on strike for better pay and conditions. You have a temporary closed for repair notice on the outside and you will open up for business as soon as you have done a repair job. (In this analogy the counsellor has legitimated the depressed client's feeling of emptiness, acknowledged the stressors in life that have brought about the emptiness and highlighted the need for the client to legitimate the meeting of their own needs and that temporarily they would have to disengage from previous activities. A useful tale has both descriptive components and prescriptive components and is an orientating metaphor for the client.)

## Panic disorder

With all the stresses you have been through you are getting a lot of unusual bodily sensations, they are unusual but not abnormal. You are rather like an old radio, it still works and one can still hear the main signal but there is a lot of crackling in the background. It is possible to become so distracted by the crackling that you do not hear the main broadcast. But on every radio there will be some background noise; on some occasions the background noise is greater than on others. The task is to learn how to develop an apathy towards the background noise and focus on the main signal. All sorts of stressors can lead to unusual sensation. There can, for example, be hormonal changes following giving birth, working long and hard, and so on. These changes are unusual in the sense that in your fifth year in school it would have been unusual for a child to have been only four foot eight or for another to have been six foot three, but children of those heights would not be abnormal. However, there would be some abnormality involved if the person was just two foot six. So many of the sensations you are experiencing are unusual, not abnormal, and what we have to make sure of is that you do not attach danger labels to these unusual sensations. It is the misinterpretation of these sensations that is largely the problem. Matters are made worse when you experience these sensations in some places and think that the place has caused the panic feelings. You therefore avoid the place, that is, you show what we call agoraphobic avoidance. We would hope to teach you that it is not the place that causes the panic symptoms.

## Generalised anxiety disorder

You keep on imagining the worst, when the worst does not happen you see yourself as being particularly lucky and then go very quickly on to imagine the worst about something else. It's as if an alarm in your body has been knocked and the alarm goes off at the slightest hassle. This state of bodily tension leads you to anticipate the worst constantly happening. Your mind races from 'what if . . .' and before you have answered you again say, 'what if . . .' and before that is answered you again say, 'what if . . .', running faster and faster on a treadmill, so that you feel that your head is coming off your shoulders. We have to teach you that your body tells you about what you have been through, rather than about what is about to happen. Your body has many false alarms and you can learn to ignore the fire drills.

Deficits in problem orientation appear particularly pronounced in clients who have borderline personality disorders or substance-abuse problems. Often clients with these difficulties do not see specific problems, rather they are conscious of their severe distress and the chaos of their lives. Relatives and friends of these clients are often acutely conscious of their difficulties and urge action upon them, but as far as action is concerned these clients are for long periods pre-contemplative, that is, they are not ready to become engaged on any actions to reach certain goals. In some instances the most a counsellor can do is to stay in contact with them, accompany them along the road rather like the pilgrims of old and in so doing affirm their worth. This offers the potential for them entering a problem-solving mode. Without a sense of worth clients are most unlikely to enter into problem solving, but there are no guarantees that even with this affirmation clients will actively begin constructing their lives. There is a tension when there is a need for audit with such clients. These clients are costly in terms of time and in giving long-term support the counsellor is reducing the number of clients to whom they could supply short-term help to produce recognisable changes. A comprehensive audit should properly identify those clients with, say, depression alone and those clients with, say, depression plus a personality disorder and then allocate them very different time scales for counselling. The author has found that about 50 per cent of patients who are clinically depressed also have a personality disorder and this appears to make a significant difference to outcome; however, if clients are suffering from an anxiety disorder the coexistence of a personality disorder does not seem to make any difference with cognitive-behavioural interventions. To be defined as having a personality disorder the patient must have begun to experience significant difficulties at least by their early twenties, these difficulties will have pre-dated any episode of anxiety or depression and the patient's difficulties must have been present in a variety of contexts, at home and at work, for example. There are diagnostic criteria for the various personality disorders in *DSM* IV (American Psychiatric Association 1994) and the counsellor ought to check the person against the criteria they see as pertinent.

Various dysfunctional beliefs are prevalent in those with deficits in problem orientation and may need to be tackled and challenged in order to enable the client to focus on problems. One of these beliefs is that any hassles are themselves a sign of the unfairness of the world and are seen as a personal affront. Teaching clients how to accept hassles, to see that they are the norm for everybody this side of the grave and that nobody is excused their supply of hassles can be very important. It is a question of asking clients why they should be excused the random unfairness that comes most people's way. To communicate such a message, however, it is important to retain the demeanour of the humble pilgrim, who may use bemused befuddlement to make the point rather than to lecture the person accompanying them.

Another common dysfunctional thought pattern is that the client sees hassles as evidence of their own personal failure and the hassles as triggers for displays of despair. This personalisation may well need to be tackled. One way of tackling this excessive sense of responsibility is to have the client locate their degree of responsibility on a scale of, say, 0–100 per cent. Alternatively, one can have the client use a responsibility pie. For example, a client who is distressed about progress on a task at work might first of all be asked to say how much their senior management are responsible for the problems because they are giving scarce resources of time and equipment. The client might conclude that half the responsibility pie is senior management's. Then they might be asked how much is their own particular manager's responsibility for the problem because he never says 'no' to his manager and always wants to keep in favour, passing everything downwards. Again, the client might conclude that a further 40 per cent of the problem is due to their own boss. This only leaves 10 per cent of the responsibility pie to the client. In this way, clients can be educated to have a more realistic appreciation of their degree of responsibility in matters. Freed from debilitating guilt clients can then begin to problem solve.

## Problem definition

Problems cannot be solved unless they are tightly defined. Imagine a patient going to see the GP and saying, 'Doctor, I am sick.' Such a statement would make life very difficult for the GP. However, if the patient indicates that their left elbow is very sore then the GP can help to begin resolving the problem. Often problems are couched in such a vague way that they defy resolution, one partner complaining about the other partner's 'general attitude' or 'unhelpful attitude', for example. Such statements evoke a sense of the client's difficulties but they are so non-specific that they cannot be addressed. In a similar way one often hears parents complaining about the misbehaviour of their toddler, making comments like 'He is just bad tempered like his father.' Again, there is little that can be done with such vague statements but if the parent was saying

'Johnny hit his little sister within half an hour of coming home from school' then one would have a sharper focus and could begin to address the difficulty, perhaps delaying the giving of a biscuit until at least half an hour after Johnny had come home from school and making it conditional on no bad behaviour in that interval.

The dominant metaphor used in cognitive-behavioural therapy is based on computers; emotional difficulties are seen as faults in information processing. Across all the emotional disorders it is possible to conceptualise the particular target problems in terms of specific maladaptive ways of thinking. The disorders highlighted earlier will be taken in turn.

## Depression

Within a cognitive-behavioural framework the defining features of depression cluster around three domains, Beck's cognitive triad (Beck et al. 1979: 11–12):

1  Negative view of self;
2  Negative view of the personal world;
3  Negative view of the future.

Most clients suffering from depression have a negative view of themselves. The more entrenched this negative view, the more difficult it is to lift the depression. The depressed client also typically has a negative view of their personal world, often feeling let down in significant relationships or feeling that they have not achieved what they should have achieved. Depressed clients have, to varying degrees, a negative view of the future: for those who have a wholly negative view of the future suicidal behaviours are a possibility. Many depressed clients have a negative view of the future but do not feel quite so totally hopeless about it as the suicidal depressed client. According to Beck et al.'s (1979) cognitive vulnerability model of depression it is not negative view of self, world and future per se that ushers in depression, but particular combinations of these with aspects of the environment. For example, if a person bases their sense of worth on the approval of others and significant important relationships fall apart then they will become depressed. However, if they were fortunate enough not to have deteriorating relationships then depression would not be ushered in. That is, there is a key and lock mechanism involved: there have to be events that are pertinent to the particular vulnerabilities for depression to occur. One type of vulnerability factor is to be what Beck terms a sociotrope, a person whose identity is totally dependant on the views and approval of others in that they do not simply like the approval of others but are in effect addicted to the approval of others. Following on from the key and lock model the sociotrope is especially vulnerable to depression if relationships break down. Beck also suggests that there is an autonomous personality who bases their sense of worth on their achievements. Such a person can function very well if they are not prevented from succeeding but if, for example, they are employed and are made redundant then in this particular context they could experience great distress. Thus targets for intervention in depression include the negative thought-content in the domains of self, personal world and the future and teaching highly sociotropic/autonomous clients how not to sabotage their lives with the worst excesses of their style. Additionally, the cognitive-behavioural counsellor will target the depressed client's information processing biases. The client is seen as using certain filter lenses and settings on a camera in order to take photographs of the situations they encounter. The cognitive-behavioural counsellor's task is to suggest that there may be other more adaptive ways of 'taking photographs' of the situation than the ones the client is currently using. Again, utilising the information-processing model, the problem-solving pilgrim is telling the client a tale about how they interact with themselves and their personal world and offering the prospect of them taking a new view of themselves. For example, some clients use a mental filter, they remember the negative of some situation and constantly replay those negative elements to themselves, distorting the whole experience. This can be conveyed to the client by saying, 'It is rather like watching *Match of the Day* on Saturday night and watching recorded highlights of only the fouls in a particular game.' Though indeed the fouls might have occurred, if the person was actually at the whole match they might have experienced a very enjoyable game. So the cognitive-behavioural strategy is not to deny negative realities but to contextualise them. Once the client becomes aware of their particular biases in information processing then they become more able to step around them.

Some depressed clients report a lifelong history of self-loathing and in these cases, they are usually also suffering from a personality disorder necessitating a tracing of the path by which their difficulties evolved. A historical perspective can often illuminate the definition of the problem. The counsellor can draw a line down a page, putting the earliest traumas, thinking and behaviour at the top with other pertinent events and associated cognitions located down the line in the order in which they occurred. For example, one of the author's clients, Tom, repeatedly self-injured. The evolution of his problems is shown in Figure 5.1. This self-injury was the presenting problem, but as can be seen, its origins lay in the past. It is often said that a picture is worth a thousand words and presenting the client's difficulties with a linear diagram makes it possible to say to the

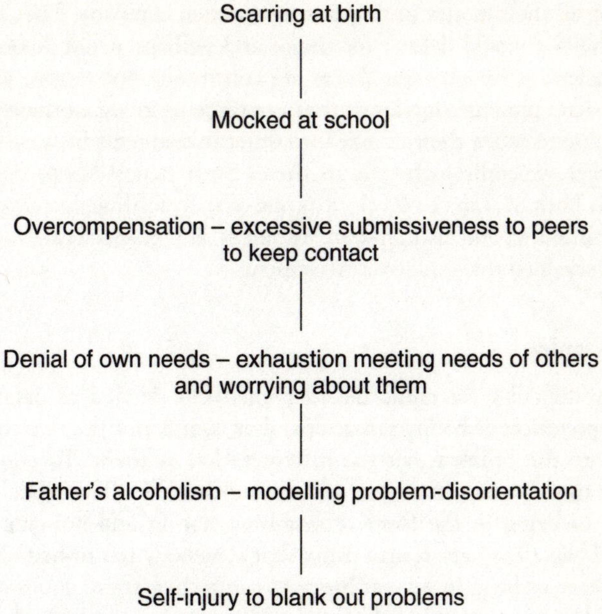

Scarring at birth

|

Mocked at school

|

Overcompensation – excessive submissiveness to peers
to keep contact

|

Denial of own needs – exhaustion meeting needs of others
and worrying about them

|

Father's alcoholism – modelling problem-disorientation

|

Self-injury to blank out problems

*Figure 5.1* The evolution of a client's difficulties

client, 'but for . . .', the subsequent problems would not have occurred. Thus in Tom's case, 'but for . . .' his being mocked at school, his present problems would probably not have arisen. This strategy acts as an antidote to the excessive self-blame that is characteristic of depression. Further, as he would not blame a young child taking on board a belief that he was fundamentally flawed and defective in his circumstances, he could come to recognise as an adult that he had, in effect, a prejudice against himself that he now needed to learn to step around. Overcoming his bigotry was made easier because he had a very good relationship with his children and his wife.

In some instances, rather than see the depressed client's difficulties in terms of thoughts it is more useful to conceptualise them at the more macro level of roles – an aggregate of thoughts, as it were. The loss of a valued role is often associated with depression. It is a common scenario amongst depressives that they have invested all their energies in one particular role; when that role no longer delivers they become depressed. For example a mother who has invested all her energies in her two young children may become depressed when they get to twelve or thirteen and are very independent. It is possible to use an investment model with clients in these situations and to suggest that they have been rather like somebody investing all their money in shares in a particular company. They believed that company would deliver for them, and perhaps it did at one stage. Nevertheless, although their shares are continuing not to give any dividend and are plummeting down, they continue to invest in the company. They refuse to move their money into other investments because they see the market generally as hostile to them. So it is possible to define the problems both at a micro level, in terms of specific thought patterns and ways of thinking, and also, in some instances, at a macro level, in terms of roles, overvalued roles and overinvestments.

## Panic disorder

The key difficulty for panic disorder clients is defined as catastrophic misinterpretation of bodily sensations, that is, it is not the sensations per se that are the problem but the interpretation of them. To convey the defining model it is possible to tell yet another tale. The model can be equated to being in the foyer of a railway station and noticing an unattended bag. One person may think that somebody has rushed off to buy a newspaper or been in a great hurry to catch their train, another person may think it is an unexploded bomb and become very frightened, backing away from the vicinity. It is the label that is put on the bag that becomes the problem rather than the bag per se. Particular catastrophic misinterpretations can take numerous forms: part of the therapist's task is to define more accurately the particular negative interpretation of symptoms, that is, in terms of the hourglass model, to define the problem more accurately. For example, one client reported that he thought he was going to faint during his panic attacks and greatly feared this. It could be easily assumed from such a fear that a central concern was that he was going to suffer considerable embarrassment as a consequence. However, further enquiry revealed that he had had a very mild stroke some two years earlier, and what he most feared was that the panic symptoms could bring on another stroke. Unlike some people with panic attacks who fear that they are going to die in a panic attack, he was not particularly bothered about dying but he was concerned that he would become severely disabled.

Negative thoughts during a panic attack can be quite different from those owned by the client outside the context of the panic attack. It is extremely important to help the client access the catastrophic misinterpretations that take place at the time of the attack. These can look extreme and strange in other situations. It is the 'hot' cognitions that are the therapeutic target rather than taking at face value the client's rational view away from the situation. Clients have usually had many panic attacks and it seems strange that these 'hot' cognitions should continue when there has been ample evidence that no catastrophe has actually befallen them. Indeed, the client can become quite annoyed with themselves for these 'hot' cognitions coming on-stream during a panic attack, and at other times would vehemently disown such beliefs. One of the reasons for the persistence of these irrational beliefs is that at the time of the attack the client often engages in safety procedures and comes to believe that they only averted a calamity because of those procedures. For example, a client who fears fainting during a panic attack might sit themselves down or hold on to someone: after the attack has passed they then believe they were only safe because of those procedures. Thus a therapeutic target is not only the 'hot' cognitions themselves but encouraging clients to give up these safety procedures and gather evidence that nothing untoward happens. Some cognitive-behaviourists approach the unusual bodily sensations from a different angle, in that they see the therapeutic target as increasing the person's tolerance of uncomfortable bodily sensations and conceptualise the client as having a phobia about their own internal bodily sensations. Within this framework clients are given strategies for increasing their tolerance of the sensations, thus, by raising the tolerance threshold, full-blown panic attacks are avoided.

## Generalised anxiety disorder

The prime target in GAD has been defined as worry and management of worry. Worry is distinguished from problem solving, which has the five stages already mentioned. In worry the client goes over the same material repetitively and switches from one topic to another before proper completion of a topic. Worry and apprehensive expectation are both sides of the same coin. It is possible to explain the role of apprehensive expectation to clients by likening the mind to a video recorder, suggesting to the client that they play and are addicted to horror videos, so that they constantly imagine the worst. It is not therefore surprising that they are distressed if they are, as it were, 'at home on a cold winter's night by themselves, with a gale blowing outside, playing the most horrific horror movie before going to bed'. In that situation they would not be surprised if they felt anxious going upstairs to bed and jumped at every noise: in a similar way it is no surprise that the anxiety sufferer feels debilitated, because they make everything they encounter into a horror movie. The goal is to wean them off their addiction to horror movies and to construct and watch reality videos, which contain in detail the most likely sequence of events, that is, those that they would be prepared to bet money on. GAD clients' thinking is dominated by Task Interfering Cognitions (TIC) which usually have an evaluative focus and are rhetorical, for example 'Have I really got what it takes?' 'What is he/she really thinking of me?' As such, they can crowd out the Task Orientated Cognitions (TOC), which are problem-solving thoughts, for example 'What exactly is the problem here?' 'What are the options ?' and so on. The therapeutic task is to teach clients to switch from TIC to TOC, utilising the mnemonic TIC/TOC.

## Experimenting with treatment components and revising them in the light of experience

A range of treatment components for depression, panic disorder and generalised anxiety is summarised in Table 5.1. It is not intended as an exhaustive list. It is beyond the scope of this chapter to go into the technical details of the treatment components and the reader is referred to Scott, Stradling and Dryden (1995), and Scott and Stradling (1998).

*Table 5.1* Treatment components for depression, panic disorder and generalised anxiety disorder

| Depression | Panic disorder | Generalised anxiety disorder |
|---|---|---|
| Activity scheduling | Hyperventilation | Worry time |
| Thought record | challenge | Time management |
| Modifying early | Avoidance of safety | Reality videos |
| maladaptive | precautions | Exercise/relaxation |
| interpretations of self | Monitoring frequency, | Coping with meta-worry |
| and others | intensity of panic and | |
| | associated cognitions | |
| | Interoceptive exposure | |

Whatever treatment component is the focus in Table 5.1 the counsellor is accompanying the client in experimenting with the strategy, they are co-investigators and as pilgrims they are of equal status. The problem-solving process necessarily involves trying some strategies that do not appear to work at all, others that are a partial success and, occasionally, some that work perfectly. Like pilgrims en route to Canterbury it is a question of edging forward and being prepared for sometimes getting lost, given the relatively rough maps we have for treating emotional disorders. Many, though, arrive happily at their destination.

# References

American Psychiatric Association (1994) *Diagnostic and Statistical Manual of Mental Disorders*. 4th edition. (*DSM IV*). Washington DC: American Psychiatric Association.

Beck, A.T., Rush, A.J., Shaw, B.F. & Emery, G. (1979) *Cognitive Therapy of Depression*. New York: Guilford Press.

British Medical Journal Publishing Group (1998) *Evidence Based Mental Health*.

Chaucer, G. (1985) *The Canterbury Tales*. Oxford: Oxford University Press.

Hammarberg, M. (1992) PENN inventory for post-traumatic stress disorder: psychometric properties. *Psychological Assessment: A Journal of Consulting and Clinical Psychology*, 4: 67–76.

Roth, A. & Fonagy, P. (1996) *What Works for Whom?* New York: Guilford Press.

Scott, M.J. & Stradling, S.G. (1998) *Brief Group Therapy: Integrating Individual and Group Behaviour Therapy*. Chichester: John Wiley & Son.

Scott, M.J., Stradling, S.G. & Dryden,W. (1995) *Developing Cognitive-Behavioural Counselling*. London: Sage Publications.

Snaith, R.P. & Zigmond, A.S. (1983) The hospital anxiety and depression scale. *Acta Psychiatrica Scandinavia*, 67: 361–370.

# 6 Establishing a therapeutic frame

*Kitty Warburton*

This chapter looks at the importance of the therapeutic frame, that is, the ground rules or boundaries of therapy or counselling, which are often taken for granted in private practice, and are sometimes sadly lacking in institutional contexts. Frequently, institutional constraints or expectations take precedence over the maintenance of the ground rules and counsellors adopt a pragmatic approach which, while making things easier for the counsellor and institution, fails the client. The chapter begins by tracing the history of the frame since Freud and looks at the theoretical arguments for maintaining a secure frame. It goes on to consider the problems inherent in maintaining the ground rules in specific institutional contexts, using some case examples. Although the theoretical orientation which pays most attention to framework and boundary issues is psychodynamic, I believe that counsellors of all orientations would do well to consider these issues when they work in institutional settings. As this chapter draws on ideas from both the psychotherapeutic and counselling perspectives, these terms are used interchangeably, as are the terms 'patient' and 'client'.

Although Freud made references to ground rules in his papers on psychoanalytic technique (Freud 1911–1915) he was notoriously lax himself in adhering to these. He used touch, confided in patients and even conducted sessions in the park (Cooper 1993). Nevertheless, he was aware of the need to provide an atmosphere of safety and to avoid gratifying the analyst's own needs (Schafer 1983). The importance of the frame or the management of the ground rules in psychotherapy has been given varying degrees of attention by analysts and therapists since.

It was Marion Milner (1952) who first used the metaphor of the frame to define the therapeutic or analytic space; to set it apart from the outside world of the client just as the frame of a painting sets it apart from the world outside. For Milner 'the frame marks off the different kind of reality that is within it from that which is outside it' (1952:183). Winnicott's notion of the analytic space being used to 'hold' the patient in a maternal way has been very influential, as has Bion's concept of 'containment' (Cooper 1993). Bleger (1967) went even further in seeing the frame as a maternal one. To him the frame is a 'permanent presence, like the parents for the child' (1967: 516) and he argued that 'a patient's frame is his most primitive fusion with the mother's body and that the psycho-analyst's frame must help to re-establish the original symbiosis in order to change it' (ibid.: 518).

## The secured frame

However, it is the communicative psychoanalyst Robert Langs who has argued most strongly for what he calls the 'secured frame' (Langs 1982). Indeed, as David Smith (1991) in his book on Langs' ideas explains, 'the structuring of the frame, the management of the ground rules, *is* the real business of psychoanalysis' (1991: 164). According to Langs, a sound or secured frame offers optimum conditions for a climate of safety and trust to develop in which the client feels free to communicate openly (Langs 1982). This 'secured frame' consists of a way of managing the ground rules of the therapeutic encounter, in order to offer:

- Total confidentiality, i.e. no notes, no tapes, no seeing of, discussion or contact with family, doctors, insurance agencies, professionals or other patients.
- Total privacy, i.e. the therapist should work from an office, not at home or at a clinic with staff and a shared waiting room, and in a soundproofed room.
- Predictability and consistency. This requires:

     a set fee which is not altered throughout the course of treatment (not no fee or reduced fees);
     a single location with an unchanged arrangement of the room;
     a set time – the day and time of the session times should be regular and remain unchanged throughout the treatment;
     a set length for all sessions – these should be exact, i.e. none longer or shorter.

- Therapist neutrality. This is demonstrated in the setting, in the therapist's manner (e.g. no touching) and the rule of abstinence, i.e. the attempt to eliminate or minimize all inappropriate gratifications for both patient and therapist.
- Therapist anonymity. That is, the therapist should not give personal opinions or indulge in self-revelation.

By adhering to these ground rules the therapist is able to create an environment of safety which fosters the development of a therapeutic alliance and is containing for both therapist and patient. When any of these ground rules is broken by the therapist, Langs (1982) refers to this as a 'frame deviation'. According to Langs, the patient responds to such deviations by producing associations which reflect unconscious judgements on the therapist's behaviour or actions. Thus, Langs argues, the patients themselves unconsciously validate the therapist's actions in holding firmly to the boundaries. It is through their ability to manage the boundaries of the therapeutic frame that therapists and counsellors are able to provide the hold and containment that patients and clients need. Langs admits that the word 'rules' can be interpreted in a mechanistic way, with an 'unfortunate penumbra of meanings' which can seem 'almost nonhuman, when in fact their very essence in the therapeutic experience is intensely human and rich in conscious and, especially, unconscious communication' (Langs 1979:13).

Of course, Langs recognised that in any clinical setting there would inevitably be many modifications to the ideal frame. Much of his work consists of supervision of trainees working in hospital clinics (see for example, Langs 1979) where few aspects of the frame are secured. However, there does need to be enough of a secured frame to contain the anxieties of both therapist and client (which in turn will help to contain the anxiety of colleagues and the institution) in order to enable the therapist to create a safe 'hold' or 'container' through which the client's 'neurosis may be insightfully resolved' (Langs 1982: 326).

## Working in institutions

In the rest of this chapter I attempt to show that as therapists and counsellors working in institutional settings we do need to pay special attention to our management of the ground rules in order to create a safe place for our clients, whether or not we work psychodynamically. This is an area that has received scant attention despite the growing demand for, and provision of, counselling and therapy in a wide range of institutions, including hospitals, primary care, schools, colleges, universities, workplaces and community settings.

I suggest that as counsellors working in such settings where it is much harder to maintain a secure frame than in private practice we need to be particularly vigilant in our management of the boundaries. Here, the temptations to change or adapt the ground rules will come from three directions: from our clients who may, on a conscious level, request that we change times of appointments or act on their behalf; from ourselves (through our own anxieties and counter-transference) and also (perhaps most importantly) from the institution itself. Of course there may be aspects of Langs' secured frame which it is impossible to adhere to in our setting, for example the set fee in an institution which offers a free service. Nonetheless, there are other aspects of the frame which we can secure in the particular setting in which we work, although we should bear in mind the conscious and unconscious responses of our clients to those aspects of the frame, such as the fixed fee, which we haven't been able to secure, as Chiefetz (1984) demonstrates in her study of clinic patients.

In attempting to maintain a secured frame for our clients we face both institutional and personal pressures; what Langs describes as 'the personal and social consequences of efforts to maintain a steady, safe, and secure environment in the face of pressures to complete insurance forms, to offer low-fee therapy and the like' (1979: xi). There are powerful needs within both the counsellor and the institution to modify the frame, to discuss clients with third parties, to vary session times and lengths and so on, which can be hard to resist.

Not only have frame issues generally been neglected by writers concerned with therapeutic work in institutions, there is also an influential body of opinion which sees counselling in specific contexts as different in kind from counselling in other contexts. Thus, for example, there is a tradition which sees 'student counselling' as a profession in its own right, with its own way of doing things, with a need for its own formal or informal code of ethics and practice, which is quite distinct from practice in a different setting (Crowther 1984; Noonan 1988; Bell 1996). In this model, the attempt is made to integrate the counselling function within the institution. The counsellor's primary responsibility is seen as being to the institution rather than to the client, and the model operates on the assumption that the interests of the institution and client are basically the same (Bond 1992). Confidentiality then becomes an institutional matter, rather than one between counsellor and client (Noonan 1988). However in arguing here the case for what Bond (1992) calls the 'differentiated model' in which the role of the counsellor is seen as essentially similar to that of the counsellor working in other settings, including private practice, and stressing the importance of maintaining appropriate boundaries, I am not suggesting that we ignore the institutional context; far from it. I am arguing that we have to pay very great attention to the special aspects of our particular context which impinge on our work. These arise daily, and it is part of our continuing struggle as counsellors to hold on to a therapeutic space when under intense pressure to deviate.

Some of the strongest pressures arise from the anxiety generated within the institution itself when faced with individuals in difficulty. Menzies Lyth (1988) has described the unconscious processes which occur in institutions which make it difficult for staff to contain their anxieties. She suggests that the operative model of many institutions may be inappropriately based on some version of the family:

> The institution may become too permissive, too non-directive, and lacking in firmness and boundary control. The staff may, in fact both lack for themselves and fail to give to clients the firm, authoritative management which is a necessary feature of both staff support and client therapy.
>
> (Menzies Lyth 1988: 230)

It is *through* maintaining firm boundaries in what is otherwise a chaotic and anxious setting that a counsellor can be most helpful to the institution at large, as well as to individual clients. Of course, initially, there will be resistance to this, especially if previous counsellors have adopted a different policy (Chiefetz 1984; Hoag 1992; Warburton 1995), or if the service has developed out of another function, for example a welfare role, and mis-understandings about the role and process of counselling will inevitably exist. But by holding firm to as secured a frame as possible and containing the initially greater anxiety generated, my own experience has suggested that there will eventually be calmer waters in which all three parties: counsellor, clients and the institution, can feel held, contained and better able to carry out their essential functions. Menzies Lyth (1988) has demonstrated the importance and the difficulties of maintaining appropriate boundaries in institutions in order to facilitate the ability of staff to carry out their tasks effectively.

Recently a number of authors have begun to consider frame issues in different contexts (although not all come to the same conclusions). These include Chiefetz (1984), Kelleher (1989), Gilbert (1989), Phillips (1991), Hoag (1992), Milton (1993), Launer (1994), Seaton (1996), Lees (1997) and an earlier version of this chapter in which I described my own struggles to provide a secured frame as a newly appointed student counsellor (Warburton 1995). Anne Gray (1994) has also written an excellent practical guide to framework issues, which I would recommend to anyone attempting to establish a secured frame counselling service within an insti-tutional context.

## Establishing a therapeutic frame

In this section I want to consider some of the special challenges and opportunities posed by working in different settings, drawing on both my own experience as a counsellor in a university as well as the experiences of some of the authors mentioned above. For simplicity I have considered four different aspects of the frame, ranging from the simpler to the more complex: place, time, conduct required and relationships. I have borrowed these categories from Molnos (1995), who in her study of brief dynamic psychotherapy emphasises the importance of handling therapeutic boundaries correctly, especially in medical settings where 'there is no general understanding of what psychotherapeutic boundaries mean and why they are necessary at all' (ibid.: 26). Molnos argues that, 'whilst some boundaries are uniquely psychoanalytic, no psychotherapy can take place without boundaries' (ibid.: 27).

## Place

In many settings it may be difficult for the counsellor to secure a suitable soundproofed room which is constantly available. Moreover, in an institutional setting the need for a quiet, private place for counselling may conflict with a desire or anxiety, both within the counselling service and the wider institution, to be more visible. For example, in universities and colleges student services departments may deliberately be situated in a central location so that they are easily accessible to students. Whilst this may be entirely appropriate, for example, for a service offering careers or welfare advice, it is not appropriate for a counselling service because it conflicts with the need for privacy. Too often establishing such a quiet, private setting for counselling, which is open to a minimum of observation, is felt, in an institutional setting, to be somehow a 'furtive, hole-in-the-corner operation' (Seaton 1996: 505), or a dumping ground for the unwanted and difficult, leading to a splitting-off of these 'bad' parts (Noonan 1988).

However, it is likely that the anxiety on the part of a counselling service in an institution to be visible in order to be recognised reflects the anxiety of workers in the rest of the organisation when faced with individuals who are distressed or in crisis. Rather than reacting to gratify such anxieties and become more visible, efforts to maintain the boundaries ultimately demonstrate to the wider setting, whether it be general practice, a university or whatever, the counsellor's or counselling service's 'capacity to hold and contain the patient's psychopathology' (Hoag 1992: 427) and thus relieve the institution of this task, so that it can concentrate on its primary task of medicine, education and so on.

Any consideration of the boundaries of place involves thinking about reception and waiting arrangements. The ideal is to have clients make their arrangements directly through the counsellor or therapist rather than via a third party, as this violates the ground rules of privacy and confidentiality (Langs 1979). In a setting where there is only one counsellor this may be possible, though it may lead to misunderstandings initially with reception staff who are used to dealing with the appointments and diaries of other workers (Hoag 1992; Warburton 1995). However, once receptionists are able to understand their role in maintaining boundaries they are less likely to feel resentful 'that their role has been usurped by the therapist who insists on keeping her own appointment book' (Hoag 1992: 427). Such arrangements mean that clients coming for first appointments with the counsellor do not have to announce themselves and their purpose in a crowded general reception/waiting area, as may happen in many medical settings (Chiefetz 1984).

## Time

The secured frame demands a set session length (normally fifty minutes) which should not vary, and a set day and time for the session which again should not vary (Langs 1979). In some institutional settings there may be pressure to vary these (Milton 1993) either for organisational reasons, for example to squeeze in more clients, or in the interests of 'flexibility'. This fails to take into account the dynamics of the counselling relationship and to provide a secure hold for clients.

To these traditional time boundaries I would add one that perhaps is even more significant: that of the ending. In her book on the dynamics of time in brief psychotherapy, Molnos demonstrates how awareness of the passage of time generates anxiety in all of us and how in psychotherapy there is a longing to recreate the timelessness of infancy and childhood. The limits set in counselling and therapy both contain and set off powerful anxieties which make it possible to work in the 'here and now' and to make links with the past (Molnos 1995).

In many institutional settings counselling is, de facto, time-limited, either by design, for example a limit of six sessions offered in general practice or an employee assistance programme (EAP), or by accident, when work terminates when term ends in an educational institution. Although it is beyond the remit of this chapter to go into any detail, there is therefore a strong argument for making this explicit and working psychodynamically with a time-limited contract, maintaining this boundary in the same way that other boundaries of time are maintained. Again there is often an anxiety (usually among counsellors and therapists whose training and personal therapy were based on a 'long-term' model) that clients are being sold short, but there is growing evidence that time-limited or brief counselling interventions can be as much or more effective than open-ended work with many client groups (Roberts 1994; Molnos 1995; Coren 1996).

## Conduct required

As Molnos points out 'the conduct required of both patient and therapist is to respect the boundaries of place and time' (1995: 29). Although, as we have seen, these boundaries are ultimately most helpful, clients (and sometimes counsellors) have an unconscious desire to disregard boundaries. Not only is there a longing to recreate the timelessness of infancy (Molnos 1995) but these boundaries generate a fear of annihilation, and ultimately of death, argues Langs (1997). Thus clients come late or early, miss sessions, request additional sessions, changes of time, and so on in an unconscious attempt to avoid or relieve their anxiety. Sometimes as therapists we make mistakes and comply with these requests, in a conscious attempt to be helpful, whilst unconsciously clients know that this is unhelpful and will tell us so through unconscious communication, for example by missing the next session or through the material they bring to it.

Some clients have particular issues around trust because of abusive past experiences, for example clients who have been sexually abused, either as children or by previous therapists, and in these cases careful attention to boundary issues is vital. In his study of sexual abuse in psychotherapy and counselling, Derek Jehu argues that subsequent therapists need to be particularly careful to maintain the framework for the therapy, 'including the punctuality and regularity of appointments and the duration of therapy' (1994:140) and to ensure that the therapy is 'made "safe" from the victim's point of view, and their boundaries are respected and not intruded upon or violated in any way' (ibid.: 139).

The other aspect of the boundary of conduct required is that of suspended action. This is often one of the most tricky boundaries for the counsellor in an institutional setting to maintain. In work settings, educational settings and in medical settings there may be pressure on counsellors to write reports of one kind or another, often to support a client's request for some other kind of help, for example a letter to support a client's request for rehousing (see Gray 1994: 68–71) or to provide 'evidence' for an examination board of 'mitigating circumstances'. Counsellors in universities are routinely expected to provide the latter, and it can be very difficult to resist such requests without feeling unhelpful or unsupportive, in what is often one of the few ways we are visible to the rest of the institution.

For example, soon after I took up my post as a counsellor in a college of higher education, a student client requested such a letter to support her request for an extension to the deadline for her dissertation. Although her previous counsellor in the institution had provided such a note in the past,

I explained to her my belief that it was not a good idea for me to get involved in this way, that is, to step outside the therapeutic relationship and to make judgements regarding the truth or otherwise of her circumstances. She understood and accepted this, as I have found clients usually do, supporting the communicative view that clients unconsciously know how the frame should be managed in psychotherapy or counselling (Smith 1991). However, on this occasion I was requested by the dean to 'support' this student by writing the note, and in fact was put under a good deal of pressure to do so. My reluctance to provide something that was seen by others as simply helpful to the student (although in fact it is more helpful to the institution, in that it absolves them from making a difficult decision on academic grounds) was not understood as these notes had been readily forthcoming in the past. Eventually, after a number of phone calls and discussions between the student's tutor, the dean, myself and her previous counsellor, I reluctantly provided the note. The situation had become chaotic and abusive, reflecting the abuse this particular client had suffered from supposedly 'caring' adults as a child. My own role had been undermined. I had stated one thing (I am your counsellor and it is not appropriate for me to act on your behalf) and done another, thus demonstrating my basic untrustworthiness to my client, who was used to having her trust abused. Hoag explains how intrusions into the therapeutic space, such as that described,

> destroy the boundaries of the therapeutic relationship and foster reactions such as mistrust, regression and acting out. They impair the intimacy necessary in a therapeutic relationship and will cause both patient and therapist to defend against the consequent loss of closeness. This defensive reaction can lead to erotic and aggressive fantasies without movement toward insight, and can destroy the therapeutic atmosphere and potential for progress.
>
> (Hoag 1992: 420)

I have tried to demonstrate to the institution the need for the counselling service to maintain a neutral stance and to pass the responsibility for decision making back to the student and the institution. As Gilbert argues:

> the counselling centre must not be viewed as a place where confidentiality is easily breached and where dispensations of various kinds are either provided or withheld. These realities are in fact synergistic. Students can safely trust that their revelations will remain contained within the therapeutic relationship. At the same time they cannot expect their counsellor to step out of those boundaries to directly

influence day-to-day matters in the client's domestic or academic life. So doing contributes to that part of the client yearning for a regressive experience in counselling, rather than for work and growth.

(Gilbert 1989: 485)

Inevitably, this is not a popular or easy stance to take, but in the long run I believe it is beneficial to students, colleagues and the institution. As time goes on and I demonstrate through my conduct and my relationships with the wider institution my perception of the counselling process, so there is a growing understanding and appreciation of what a counselling service can, and cannot, offer and the inappropriate demands and anxieties subside. At the same time the service becomes more highly regarded by students, who can be sure that we will retain our neutrality, and by colleagues, who increasingly recognise the effectiveness of the service. Hoag (1992) describes a similar process taking place in the medical setting in which she works.

If we fail to maintain these particular boundaries the counselling service is likely to be sucked into an administrative vacuum (Gilbert 1989) and the institution will put increasing pressure on the counselling service to carry out disciplinary functions. Another client, G, was sent to the counselling service as a condition of being allowed to retake her final teaching practice. At our first meeting G produced a letter from her tutor laying down this condition and requiring confirmation from the counselling service of her attendance. She was suspicious of the college counselling service and ambivalent about counselling, yet felt forced to attend. Over seven sessions we continually worked on these feelings, although at the same time we were able to make some links between what had happened during her own schooldays and her subsequent difficulties with teaching practice, and also with her relationship with her mother. However, the work was patchy and I feared that the therapeutic alliance had been fatally undermined by the circumstances of her referral. However, a couple of months after concluding our work together, G rang me to request a return to counselling. This time there was no ambivalence and our work together was productive and successful.

### Relationships

As Molnos (1995) points out, many clients put us under enormous pressure to change our relationship with them from a therapeutic one to a social one, for example by asking personal questions, bringing presents, and so on, and it is a key feature of psychodynamic work to abstain from self-disclosure. In an institutional context, however, there are also relationships with other staff members to consider. There may be concepts of teamwork (as in general practice or in student services departments) which also put us under great pressure to adapt or dismantle our boundaries. In addition, there is often pressure on us to wear more than one 'hat', such as the counsellor who is also expected to act as receptionist on occasion; the student counsellor who is expected to provide welfare advice or the work-place counsellor who is also required to administer the benevolent fund. There are practice nurses and even general practitioners who counsel their patients. In a paper exploring the difficulties inherent in his dual role as GP and counsellor, Kelleher (1989) concluded that for him, as a GP, to offer his services as a counsellor to his patients 'smacks of deviant frame therapy' and would be very confusing for the client. Whatever context we work in our clients need to feel safe: if they know or suspect that we will consult with other members of staff then this damages, undermines and may even destroy any potential for therapeutic work. We therefore need to work hard to contain the anxieties of our colleagues whilst providing a therapeutic space for our clients, and we need to be aware of the unconscious processes that take place in institutions and make it hard for staff (including ourselves) to contain such anxieties (Menzies Lyth 1988).

Menzies Lyth has demonstrated that many institutions tend to operate as an anxious, rather enmeshed family, as the following case example may illustrate. When M, a young man in his first year, came to see me he was having difficulties both in coping with his teaching course and in his interpersonal relationships. He was angry and defensive and distrustful of counselling but had come because of pressure from his tutors and because it seemed to be his last hope. Between his second and third session his tutor contacted me to discuss his concerns about M. When M came to his third session he began by saying 'I suppose you've been hearing things about me.' He had decided that counselling was not going to help after all, and that he would 'just try to get on with things'. He left the session early and made no further contact. However I had several phone calls from tutors anxious about M, wanting to know what could be done – feeling that he desperately needed 'help'. Although I was careful not to discuss M in any detail, I nevertheless felt uneasy at these conversations and very aware of a powerful and uncomfortable conflict between my own anxiety to be seen to be doing a 'good job' in the eyes of my colleagues and my wish to work within the boundaries of the therapeutic role. Hoag (1992) describes similar conflicts in her work as a general practice counsellor. In these circumstances I attempted, as May (1988:19) has suggested, to 'reflect on and help contain anxieties, rather than to internalize the fears and rush to fulfill the initial request'. In attempting to allay the anxiety of staff I suggested that it may not be possible to do anything if the student does not want help. The staff then had to take difficult decisions regarding his continuing on the course on academic and behavioural grounds. However it is vital to distinguish, as May (1988) points out, between the 'administrative (or academic) voice' which needs to be able to say 'no' on behavioural or academic grounds and the 'psychotherapeutic voice' which suspends judgement, listens and attempts to understand.

## Conclusion

In this chapter I have argued for the need to maintain appropriate boundaries for clinical work in institutional settings and in so doing I am very much aware that this tends to go against current trends to integrate with colleagues from different disciplines and to adapt our work to fit in with the established ethos and mores of the setting in which we work (Noonan 1988; Bond 1992). It seems to me that as a relatively new profession we have a tendency to be too apologetic. We feel insecure and suspect that it is all too easy for managers looking to make operational savings to cut or do away with the counselling service; we therefore try to keep everyone happy even if in some cases this jeopardises the therapeutic work that is our primary reason for being there. We thus feel obliged to make ourselves more visible, sometimes to the detriment of our credibility as practising counsellors (Bell 1996).

Although it will be impossible in most institutional settings to provide a totally secured frame, as Smith (1991) points out, 'there is always scope for some securing of the frame' even in the most unsympathetic environment. 'These are called *secured frame moments* and will have constructive effects despite the presence or even preponderance of contradictory factors' (Smith 1991: 191).

According to Langs (quoted in Smith 1991: 173), these constructive effects offer the patient:

- A sense of basic trust;
- Clear interpersonal boundaries between patient and therapist creating both appropriate distance and intimacy and thus making the relationship safe and secure;
- Unconscious support for the patient's contact with reality and his or her capacity to test reality;
- The foundation for a relationship that entails a healthy therapeutic symbiosis;
- The basis for a mode of cure that will take place through genuine insight and not entail relief through action-discharge;

- A situation in which the unfolding dynamics will centre on the patient's madness rather than the madness of the therapist;
- An unconscious image and introject of the therapist as having a sound identity and an inner state of healthy narcissistic balances;
- An image of the therapist as sane;
- A powerful sense of being held well and of appropriate containment;
- A situation of appropriate frustration and healthy satisfactions.

Much of the discussion in this chapter has been drawn from the psychodynamic tradition. However I would argue, with Molnos (1995), that careful attention to these boundary issues is just as important for counsellors working from different theoretical viewpoints. A secured frame offers a 'special place' carved out from everyday life in which the therapeutic process (however this is defined) may take place (Molnos 1995). This special place creates an atmosphere of safety in which clients are free to explore aspects of themselves and their difficulties and work towards resolving them without feeling judged or fearing that confidences will be broken.

# References

Bell, E. (1996) *Counselling in Further and Higher Education*, Buckingham: Open University Press

Bleger, J. (1967) 'Psychoanalysis of the psycho-analytic frame', *International Journal of Psycho-Analysis* 48: 511–519

Bond, T. (1992) 'Ethical issues in counselling in education', *British Journal of Guidance and Counselling* 20: 51–63

Cheifetz, L. (1984) 'Framework violations in psychotherapy with clinic patients', in J. Raney (ed.) *Listening and Interpreting: The Challenge of the Work of Robert Langs*, London: Jason Aronson, 215–253

Cooper, J. (1993) 'Different ways of structuring the frame: according to Winnicott, Khan and Langs', *Journal of the British Association of Psychotherapists* 24: 23–35

Coren, A. (1996) 'Brief therapy – base metal or pure gold?', *Psychodynamic Counselling* 2: 22–38

Crowther, R.H. (1984) 'Is student counselling a profession?', *British Journal of Guidance and Counselling* 12: 124–131

Freud, S. (1911–1915) *Papers on Technique*, Standard Edition 12, London: Hogarth Press/Institute of Psycho-Analysis

Gilbert, S. (1989) 'The juggling act of the college counselling centre: a point of view', *The Counselling Psychologist* 17: 477–489

Gray, A. (1994) *An Introduction to the Therapeutic Frame*, London: Routledge

Hoag, L. (1992) 'Psychotherapy in the general practice surgery: considerations of the frame', *British Journal of Psychotherapy* 8: 417–429

Jehu, D. (1994) *Patients as Victims*, New York: Wiley

Kelleher, D. (1989) 'The GP as counsellor: an examination of counselling by general practitioners', *British Psychological Society Psychology Section Review* 4: 7–13

Langs, R. (1979) *The Therapeutic Environment*, New York: Jason Aronson

Langs, R. (1982) *Psychotherapy: A Basic Text*, New York: Jason Aronson

Langs, R. (1997) *Death Anxiety and Clinical Practice*, London: Karnac

Launer, J. (1994) 'Psychotherapy in the general practice surgery: working with and without a secure therapeutic frame', *British Journal of Psychotherapy* 11: 120–126

Lees, J. (1997) 'An approach to counselling in GP surgeries', *Psychodynamic Counselling* 3: 33–48

May, R. (1988) 'Boundaries and voices', in R. May (ed.) *Psychoanalytic Psychotherapy in a College Context*, New York: Praeger, 3–21

Menzies Lyth, I. (1988) *Containing Anxiety in Institutions*, London: Free Association Books

Milner, M. (1952) 'Aspects of symbolism in comprehension of the not-self', *International Journal of Psycho-Analysis* 33: 181–195

Milton, M. (1993) 'Counselling in institutional settings – secure frame possibility or not?', *Counselling* 4: 284–286

Molnos, A. (1995) *A Question of Time: Essentials of Brief Dynamic Psychotherapy*, London: Karnac

Noonan, E. (1988) 'The impact of the institution on psychotherapy', in R. May (ed.) *Psychoanalytic Psychotherapy in a College Context*, New York: Praeger, 41–54

Phillips, M. (1991) 'Violations of the ground rule of confidentiality in a counselling centre: the contribution of Langs', *Counselling* 2: 92–94

Roberts, J. (1994) 'Time-limited counselling', *Psychodynamic Counselling* 1: 93–105

Schafer, R. (1983) *The Analytic Attitude*, London: Hogarth Press

Seaton, S. (1996) 'Introducing counselling in secondary schools: a case study with reference to frame issues', *Psychodynamic Counselling* 2: 498–512

Smith, D. (1991) *Hidden Conversations: An Introduction to Communicative Psychoanalysis*, London: Tavistock/Routledge

Warburton, K. (1995) 'Student counselling: a consideration of ethical and framework issues', *Psychodynamic Counselling* 1: 421–435

# 7  The therapeutic space and relationship

*Alison Vaspe*

I work as a counsellor in two settings which, despite their shared world of medicine, have two different primary tasks. In one, this task is teaching students to be doctors and dentists; in the other, it is treating and caring for patients in a general practice. I have found my experience in each to have some areas in common, and some areas that are distinctively coloured by the different setting and task. In this chapter, I want to write about how I make therapeutic space and relationships within these two organizations.

My perspective is that of a counsellor trained to draw upon psychodynamic theories to think about both work with individual clients and the context in which that work takes place. My orientation is independent within the object-relations tradition, which means for me that I draw upon the theories of a range of theorists and also try to keep abreast of contemporary developments in psychoanalytic thinking. My main influences are Klein and Winnicott and the development of their ideas by feminists working psychoanalytically, for example Jessica Benjamin and the practitioners who have come out of the Women's Therapy Centre. I have also benefited greatly from being trained on a course which teaches organizational dynamics as an integral part of the counsellor's work. In this chapter, I will try to show how my thoughts and feelings about these dynamics have a central place in any attempt to provide a therapeutic space and relationships at work.

## Potential Space

'Potential Space' is Winnicott's term for an arena in which a particular kind of emotional experience can take place (1991). Winnicott located this originally between mother and baby, but extended it into other relationships as well, notably the therapeutic one and that between the individual and culture, art or society. The Potential Space is not situated within the individual psyche, nor in the 'shared reality' of two people, but 'at the border of both and both contribute to it . . . It is the space that initially both joined and separated the baby and the mother whose reliability and love gave a sense of trust and confidence in the environmental factor . . . it is the third area of experience in which spontaneous action, imagination and creativity in its widest sense activate self-experiences of feeling "real"' (Tonnesmann 1993: 11–12).

Potential Space is a useful concept for counsellors who believe in the need to be attentive to the dynamics of both the individual client and the setting. It reminds me that both client and setting have an effect on me. My response is at the same time subjective and objective – or, as Winnicott has it, I experience them in two ways, as 'the subjective object and [as] the object objectively perceived' (1991: 100). For example, in both of the settings in which I work, the guiding dynamic principles could be said to be action and authority. Both centre on medical treatment, though in one the primary task is teaching and in the other it is caring for patients as one member of a multi-disciplinary team. In thinking about my work in relation to these primary tasks, I have found myself considering the kind of activity that goes on in a counselling session, and the way in which it differs from medical treatment.

I recall walking one morning into the hospital where I work as a student counsellor. In front of me was a group of medical students. I didn't know any of them, but it was quite clear to me that they were medical students. I wondered why, and thought it wasn't just the youthfulness or the territorial confidence that made people around them look somehow blurred, or less defined, or ordinary; I watched the way they walked and carried themselves and thought, 'Oh yes, of course, they're being taught to *do* things to people.'

The temptation, then, was to define therapeutic work as the antithesis of *doing* – to recall how Freud 'changed the traditional authoritarian doctor–patient relationship into a *partnership* to which both analyst and patient contribute on equal terms but with different tasks' (quoted in Tonnesmann 1993: 4). However, I also think that my spontaneous thought was in some way a caricature, arising from my feelings about the way emotional life is often accorded second place in these organizations. Doctors do not just *do* things to patients; they also negotiate treatments and talk through personal issues with them. Neither can the counselling relationship be said to be entirely free of power imbalance. And counsellors, by the way they talk with and see their clients, are certainly in a sense *doing* something to them, and especially to the material they are brought. So, on reflection, the question became one of how to conceptualize the two different kinds of doing in a way that avoided counselling becoming, by default, and in relation to the active and stereotypically male medical model of treatment, a passive, 'feminine', activity. As Tara Weeramanthri describes it, one of the pitfalls for women in the caring professions is of 'being misunderstood as an emotional "sponge", soaking up everything that comes in one's direction, as if just being there and taking it is necessarily helpful to the client' (1997: 216).

Perhaps this is one boundary that the concept of a Potential Space may help to keep: a boundary that does not present a straightforward choice between doing or being done to, but rather provides an arena for a third area of experience. This boundary, in other words, may offer a way out of a stereotyped view of gender in which the male is equated with action and the female with the passive – in which men 'do' and women are done to. It may then be possible to allow a concept of therapeutic space in which intuition, empathy and thought can be recognized as active processes rather than mere passive receptacles. In such a space, the counsellor's reflections upon, or 'mirroring' of, what the client is saying and feeling can be seen as an active process, by which change can come about.[1]

### Holding the Potential Space in an organizational setting

Both the work of counselling students and that of counselling patients tends to be mainly short term. Students present in crisis before exams, or after failing them, or when fearful of breakdown, or when their depression can no longer be denied or their friends have simply had enough. There are opportunities for longer-term work where necessary and appropriate, but for the most part brief counselling is the order of the day. Patients at the health centre where I work go through a more structured process which begins in consultation with their GP, and then involves a referral being sent to the counselling service, there to await the patient's own application: only when both forms meet is an appointment offered. None the less, these patients are more than likely to have reached their own point of crisis, and the maximum number of sessions we have to offer for therapeutic work is twelve at weekly or fortnightly intervals, or about the same number spread over a year or so. How, one may ask, can the concept of space apply here, with its connotations of freedom, ease, ability to breathe?

I believe the main condition for this kind of space lies in the counsellor's ability to be aware of the unconscious life and dynamics, not just of the individual client, but of the organization as well. For both, she will need to find a space in which she can feel, think about and reflect upon what is going on. In other words, I try to create a Potential Space within the organization by reflecting on my own experience of subjective perception, using my senses, impressions and expectations or imaginings, and also by trying to stay in touch with what is going on in the organization as a whole – with the kind of objective reality that can be agreed upon by two individuals. If I can occupy this boundary between subjective and objective experience, then I am more likely to be able to offer the 'safe, maternal holding' that the feminist psychoanalyst Jessica Benjamin has identified as necessary for exploration and discovery of feelings to occur without 'impingement, intrusion or violation' (1990: 128).

Organizations have many features that can be distracting or testing for the counsellor–client relationship. Unlike in most private work, the counsellor can be seen in company with the equivalent of partners or siblings, in the form of colleagues (other support workers, whether counsellors, welfare officers or receptionists, or members of the medical or psychiatric staff), and also parents in the form of her employers. Coupled with the role of the counsellor in relation to the primary task of the organization, with its implications of relative status and of how counselling relates to and is located among these other central tasks, and the possibilities for certain kinds of feelings typically to arise can be seen almost as inevitable: does a referral mean, for example, that the client is weak, mad or a failure, a hypochondriac whose physical illness is not taken seriously, or a difficult customer? On the other hand, the situation within an organization can also provide a sense of containment and structure for a client (here, counselling goes on; there, life in the organization carries on as usual). There may be a sharper sense of relevance, in that counselling contributes to the ongoing primary task of the organization, helping students to study and learn and patients to recover from ill health or 'dis-ease'. Equally, for the counsellor, the different perspectives and information offered by colleagues involved in different tasks make it possible to stay in touch with the life of the organization and to keep a sense of relative importance and proportion. However, when the organization and the dynamics of its everyday life are not borne in mind and reckoned with, organizational factors can influence the counsellor in a negative way, which can impinge, intrude upon and violate the therapeutic space.

I do not, therefore, take the line that the space must be protected from impingement by the counsellor keeping apart from the setting. Rather, I believe that it is essential to ensure the space she provides is therapeutic not just with regard to the physical constancies of time, place, privacy and presence. At least as important, if not more so, is the ability of the counsellor to be able to concentrate wholeheartedly on her client: to be able to breathe and move, mentally. This may not be possible if organizational dynamics are not known about and processed.

As an example, I should like to describe an experience I had fairly recently of sudden self-awareness. It took the form of a powerful revelation, and not a particularly pleasant one, but it felt like a kind of epiphany – something found, but also re-found, one of those moments in life when you find yourself revisiting a place that is all too familiar. The occasion for this experience was a request to provide a group for some students who had failed their finals.

One issue that a student counsellor has to be able to process is the competitiveness of working in a learning environment (Bell 1997: 202–203). This may be more true of student life in the 1990s than previously (Heyno 1996: 6–8). Certainly I have found the setting of a medical school to be a highly competitive place, which I attribute partly to the academic requirements of a long and taxing training, and also to the anxiety that attaches to success and failure in a context in which these can stand for life and death – the reality of a doctor's life for which the exams sometimes seem to stand. Hence the feelings that accompany success and failure are extremely powerful.

I became aware of this with one of the first students I saw, a very bright young dental student who was passing exam after exam. He probably came across in class as studious, maybe rather quiet, a bit of a 'little professor', but none the less as someone who fitted in: certainly he had many friends. In counselling, however, he spoke of a profound depression and a desire to be 'nice' which left him with nowhere to direct his aggressive feelings other than towards himself, in the form of suicidal thoughts. With him in mind I would say to personal tutors, who in our meetings would always tend to focus on students who had failed exams, that it was not just students who failed who needed help; sometimes the successful students had serious emotional difficulties too. This was a valid point, and my aim was to shift the focus of tutors away from purely academic concerns and towards students' emotional wellbeing. However, when I was asked to run a group for the students who had failed their finals, I realized how much I also wanted to dissociate myself from failure.

I had initially run groups for students resitting exams with a colleague in the Education Development Unit. After a while, we began to run groups for particular students facing key exams – not just the resits. Now, I was shocked to find how little I wanted to sit with the painful experience of failure that these students were faced with after five, sometimes six, years of work. In the group I found myself feeling the strain of containing my own emotions, in particular a strong desire to deny reality. The word 'failure' proved the sticking point, and not just for me. My colleague had written the letter announcing the group without mentioning the word ('lack of success' was her term), while for my part I found myself thinking of the *Fawlty Towers* episode in which John Cleese's hotel manager, faced with a party of Germans, keeps telling himself not to mention the war, and then of course does so at every turn, in the most clumsy and offensive way imaginable. It was difficult to stay in touch with the shock, the sense of inadequacy and self-hatred of the students. That I could do so to some extent was thanks to preliminary work in supervision, and to a memory that came to me shortly beforehand, of a strong sense of failure in myself, which at one point had dominated my life and which I was now in danger of projecting into the very group of people who needed to project their unmanageable feelings into me.

My fear and denial were not created by the university, but fed in to a social defence against being marked out by the organization as a 'dumping-ground' for failure. Isabel Menzies Lyth has shown how social defences form, and has located them in the realm of paranoid–schizoid defence systems. One characteristic of such defences is that 'they prevent true insight into the nature of problems and realistic appreciation of their seriousness' (Menzies Lyth 1988: 81). This is not just an issue for one particular exam group. In a climate where failure and death are taboo, where staff live in fear of being associated with one or the other and are at the same time suffering from job insecurity and their own rivalries and instinct for survival, individual students' fears can have no opportunity to be heard and made less toxic. The result is denial of a frightening and damaging kind, and counselling may be the only place where the fears can be voiced, provided the counsellor is not too paralysed by her own fears and insecurities to listen – or, to return to the metaphor of active reflection, to 'mirror' for the client experiences that they can recognize as their own, rather than imposing the counsellor's 'own feelings of being accused and persecuted' (Ernst 1987: 71).

This experience underlined for me how important it is that the counselling service, while remaining private, confidential and boundaried, should not allow itself to be cut off from the context in which it operates, as though it has nothing to do with the organization's primary task. Each organization, I believe, will raise different issues for the counsellor, and the extent to which she can be aware of herself in relation to the structure, dynamics and institutional defences against anxiety will correspond to the extent to which the space she creates between herself and her client is therapeutic.

Having touched on some issues around the therapeutic space, I shall now look within the space, at the relationship between the participants in the counselling dialogue.

### Holding the therapeutic relationship within the organization: brief work

Often, the counselling dialogue in organizations has to take account of a third party. In the general practice setting, this is usually the GP who referred the patient. To illustrate some issues that can arise in this context, I will draw upon my experience with Mr M, an African refugee who had been imprisoned and tortured in his country and given political asylum in Britain. He was now suffering nightmares, depression and insomnia.

Mr M had built up a relationship with his GP involving regular visits and perhaps some shared sense of identity arising from the fact that both were from ethnic minority groups, although the GP was a British-Asian woman and he was a black African man living in a foreign country. Looking at the notes before we met, I could see a developing communication between them. They had talked more than once about counselling, and it seemed a good referral. However, when I met him for an assessment session, he was silent and seemed uncomfortable. He seemed to feel he had been directed to come, and wanted to talk about some form of medication that would help him sleep without being disturbed by nightmares. He did describe the terrifying nightmares, in which he was in fear of his life, and I tried to tell him that he could come to me to talk about his fears as well as continuing to see his GP – it was not a case of either/or. However – and this may partly have been due to my own fears about what he would tell me about his experiences of imprisonment and torture – I felt he was not ready to talk, and in fact he did not turn up for his next appointment.

The GP encouraged him to persevere, and after some weeks Mr M approached the service again. I offered him another appointment as soon as I could. This time it seemed that my room – a narrow, barrel-vaulted, white and rather cell-like space – was disturbing to him. He became very frightened and agitated and several times looked fearfully over his shoulder. I found it very hard to make myself understood, or to find words that would express what he was showing me of his fear. All I could do was identify a link between the nightmares he was having at night, his imprisonment and torture in Africa, and what he was showing me now: to bring the nightmare into the room and show I was prepared to re-experience something of it with him. I was encouraged by my supervisor to offer an interpreter, and to say I might be able to find another, less cell-like, room, but when I suggested this in his next session, he said he did not wish me to do either. It was, he said, just to be 'you and me – no one else'.

The sessions we had together were difficult and uncomfortable, even though I decided to limit them to thirty minutes rather than fifty. Fifty minutes did seem to be too long for him, but I was also unsure whether I would be able to sustain the longer period of time. I felt all wrong – ignorant of the politics of his country and his language, reminding him instead of his arrival in London, surrounded by anonymous white faces, people 'always busy', rushing through the streets around him. I also had difficulty in imagining, or wanting to imagine, what he had been through. I was ashamed of my cowardice and my inexperience of working with someone badly traumatized.

Now, I think my fears and discomfort, while undoubtedly my own, also had relevance for his experience of being in exile from the known and familiar, from a taken-for-granted milieu of language and understanding, and the isolation of terrifying memories. Then, I could no more have put that need into words than he could have. Again, supervision helped, and was essential in identifying the strand of loss that ran through his recent life.

Slowly, painstakingly, we began to shape a relationship in which he could talk about his experience. He continued to have moments of being overtaken by fear in the room, but gradually we began to address the losses he had experienced: his home, from which he was in exile; his family, unable to come to the UK to visit him; his hopes of success as a promising young student; his fiancée. He began to speak of arranging a meeting with his mother in a neutral country, and I began to feel some hope that he might be able to find a way to live in London that would be less lonely and cut off. Then he was offered accommodation in another part of London, which meant he had to leave the practice.

During the last session Mr M spoke of his gratitude towards the health centre and his sorrow at leaving. He had tears in his eyes, and I felt close to tears myself. His sad farewell was to the health centre as a whole, which had provided him with a place to be with his physical and emotional pain, as well as to me as his counsellor. He had been in the care of a team consisting of the GP, of the counsellor and also the receptionist who saw him as a 'lost soul' and went out of her way to offer him assistance and a warm greeting. Outside that safe structure of everyday care and containment, I believe counselling would have been too frightening and destabilizing.

This case taught me much about forming relationships in the general practice setting. It underlined the need to find my part in a multi-disciplinary team in which the members offer different areas of expertise but a combined form of care. This can raise issues of interdisciplinary rivalry or envy of different tasks. It was hard, for example, not to want to act the GP, not to be able to relieve Mr M's physical pain, but to have to sit with him in a bare room, relying on what words we could find between us.

Finally, this case illustrates for me the need to work with the limitations of the organization. In this case, while the care we offered met Mr M's needs very well for the time he lived in the area, the offer of better accommodation outside the health authority boundaries could not be denied. It was necessary to acknowledge the reality of this in order to find a sense of closure – even if the ending felt premature, so that it was with a sensation of almost physical pain that I watched Mr M walk away for the last time.

### Holding the therapeutic relationship within the organization: longer-term relationships

As well as short-term counselling in organizational settings, longer-term relationships sometimes need to be made available for a client's emotional and relationship issues to be worked through. Again, however, the organization is always there. At times the therapeutic relationship is directly at issue, as emotional sticking points get acted out in other areas; at other times, the counsellor's different involvements with the organization overlap with her one-to-one relationship with the client.

For example, I mentioned above the understandable tendency of teaching staff to focus on exams as a gauge of a student's general wellbeing. A parallel focus with students was on what they called, variously, 'coping techniques', or 'stress management'. They seemed to want and expect their feelings of being unmotivated, or wound up, or depressed to be dealt with very quickly, as though one counselling session should effectively 'fix it'. On the other hand, when they spoke in detail about their difficulties, it was apparent that they were not going to be easily fixed, and, moreover, that they had delayed coming to counselling for some time – in a few instances, for years. By the time they arrived in my room, they were often in a bad way, and sometimes seemed to have reached a point of feeling hopeless and despairing. They felt, many of them, a very long way from home, or from any thought that a listening ear could help them. My way of thinking about their difficulties, which often seemed to strike a chord, none the less seemed to fall short of the intervention they had hoped for.

The difficulty, I realized, lay with the maternal transference. That is, I found I was very quickly identified with a mother figure, so that the qualities attributed to their real-life mothers when the students first described for me their home life and relationships soon seemed to attach to me. Often, on presentation, these qualities were quite negative. It felt as though the expectation of counselling was that it would not be able to help. Often I felt a useless woman – not medically trained, lacking the skill to cure them or remove their stumbling blocks, and in danger either of functioning as a kind of emotional dustbin for their feelings of inadequacy and failure, or, worse, of offering a relationship that would be experienced as 'regressively frightening . . . or comforting' (Coren 1996: 29). If counselling was to be helpful to the student, this low expectation of the counsellor had to be tackled at once. On the other hand, I did not want to become infected by the organizational dynamic and end up lecturing students about their problems. It was this dilemma that led me to reconceptualize counselling for myself, to rediscover the therapeutic space as a place for 'active reflection', avoiding the stereotypical male = active/ female = passive equation. With this in mind, I should like to end by thinking about Gina, a medical student who came to me early in her training feeling 'homesick, lonely and paranoid'.

Gina described a difficult family set-up: her father, a doctor, was very much the paternal authority, while her mother was described disparagingly as 'a part-time teacher' (this to a part-time counsellor) who was 'miserable' and 'clinging'; she also had an older sister who seemed to have quite serious emotional problems. Her memories of childhood resembled isolated snap-shots, seen but not felt, rather than bringing to light relationship issues that we could focus on in the counselling. She was tearful and wretched and thinking of throwing in her training. Her end of term exams were approaching, and she had thoughts of deliberately failing and getting out that way. She was only doing it for her father, she said. She didn't fit in, and anyway nothing ever changed, so what was the point of trying?

Gina came for regular sessions for the next eight months, including during holiday periods. I asked her to see her doctor to begin with, as her exams were close and I was concerned that she had reached a point of feeling depressed. He thought her mood low but did not think anti-depressants were called for. In counselling, over these eight months, Gina completed the first stage of her training, and then decided to defer the next step and instead gain an academic qualification.

In those months, the central theme was her relationship with her mother. I came to understand how Gina's attempts to merge with her, and at the same time turn her into a person of no importance, blocked her own development, so that, indeed, 'nothing changed'. As she talked of her choice of medicine as a career it became clear to what extent she had made this choice to please her father, but also that it tuned in with her desire to play a 'leading role' – to be a star, rising above the low mood of her quite depressed sounding family attachments, particularly to her mother. Counselling, which put her in touch with these everyday low feelings within herself, and with the difficulties of being at the start of a long and difficult training which had been chosen for quite mixed reasons, was attacked on various fronts, many of them on 'maternal' grounds. When we came close to sad, dejected feelings, it was laughed at or made to seem 'dull and dowdy' – as though she was coming for a depressed and clinging mother, rather than with any expectation of change for herself. When my first holiday break came up, she went to the medical school psychiatrist and was furious when this 'father' said she was not depressed and wrote to me as her counsellor with an assessment of her psychiatric state. When the Education Advisor and I offered an exam preparation group for her year, she felt jealous, as she did when her mother made a point of praising her sister for her struggles to succeed academically, while Gina, 'the clever one', was expected to carry on working and succeed. Equally, when she passed her exams and was preparing to leave the college, and hence the counselling, she was pleased to think she would have 'something to take away', in the form of the degree she was aiming for, while counselling felt very much the poor relation, good only for doing her dirty washing, as when she greeted her mother with an armful of laundry after a holiday.

The danger for the counselling lay in the possibility that she might succeed in turning me into a depressed mother-figure – and indeed in her sessions it was difficult to think, and not to feel sleepy and baffled at her rather droning manner of speaking and the perpetual worrying away at herself – or that she would succeed in splitting the counselling off from her training by playing one 'parent' off against the other. When the counselling survived, she was faced with a terrible inner loneliness, which was compounded by her envy and competitiveness when anyone proved themselves able to do something she could not. In this case, the envy was of a counsellor who could think about her problems and show her what she was doing to herself. It was painful for her to see how she repeatedly destroyed what she was offered by those around her, but gradually she did manage to hold on to some sense of her own potential, and to find a way forward that she could sustain.

The everyday links with Gina's life in the organization seemed to generate a series of tests for the counselling. However, they also provided a rhythm that allowed it to tune in to the rhythm of her student world. It became possible to link counselling with her life of exams and learning in a way that seemed helpful to her. For example, before one set of exams, she took some time to 'revise' what she had learnt about herself through counselling and to rehearse the ending of our relationship. Halfway through the counselling, she formed a pop group with some other students and was able to enjoy a degree of 'stardom' as a singer in it. When another singer joined the band she was surprised to find she did not feel threatened, but thought that, just as sometimes in counselling we were both able to think about her, so perhaps they could sing together 'in harmony' (though she worried she might sound flat). Finally, in relation to her choice of profession, she moved from her early daydreams of being a 'doctor like the doctors on TV', heroically curing the sick and rescuing the injured, but not wanting to do the 'boring' work of learning, to thinking that perhaps she might work as a surgeon: she thought she would like to 'mend wounds' and that that would prove a quiet and methodical way of working, reminiscent of the days when she used to enjoy sewing in her room.[2]

I began by referring to Winnicott, and would like to return to him on ending. It seems to me that his concept of a 'third area of experience', with its connotations of 'safe, maternal holding' and protection from intrusion and impingement, has much to offer counsellors in organizational settings. Often, one is dealing with a first encounter with psychological help. It may feel very strange to be in a room with a counsellor in a place generally associated with study or implicitly physical health care. It may represent a sense of failure (no one else can help me), madness, or last resort. But, by its existence within these settings, counselling may indicate an acknowledgment on the part of the organization of a third dimension to the working relationships that occur there. The end result may be an enrichment of those relationships. Thus, counselling in organizations can, I believe, provide a means of developing an awareness of the Potential Space within that organization, in which the fears, anxieties and subjectivity of its members may be acknowledged. I have therefore tried to show some areas in which counselling overlaps with the organization as a whole, and some of the ways that I try to relate to the outer life of the organization, as well as to the inner life of the individual psyche in the course of counselling. I have described some of the difficulties I have found in occupying this space and have indicated that, not only is supervision of essential value, but that as a counsellor I have depended upon the kind of self-knowledge that can only be gained through the exploration of thoughts and feelings in a safe, therapeutic space of one's own.

## Acknowledgements

I am grateful to my colleagues for helping me to see and play my part in the organizations we work in: Diana Bass, Nigel Burch, Trudy Chapman, Dr Mary Herns, Romayne Jesty, Adrian Lenthall and Roz Rome. I should also like to thank Mary Banks, Sheila Ernst, Marilyn Miller-Pietroni and Paul Terry for all they have taught me as well as for their comments on this chapter. Finally, I am grateful to Dr Gertrud Mander for helping me find my own Potential Space, and to my husband, Peter Vaspe, for helping me to keep it.

## Notes

1 I was interested to find that this concept is borne out in physics. Newton's third law of mechanics gives the principle: 'Whenever a body exerts a force on another body, the latter exerts a force of equal magnitude and opposite direction on the former.' The same principle accounts for the phenomenon of the reflection of light off a surface. The reflection is the effect of the action of the light in conjunction with the action of the surface. I have my nephew, Ralf Vaspe, to thank for this observation.

2 The implications for women of studying medicine are fascinating and complex, and cannot be done justice to in this chapter. However, it was interesting to note that this was the first time that medicine had been seen in gendered terms that related less to traditionally masculine areas than to a more traditionally female activity, and to her own childhood.

## References

Elsa Bell (1997) 'Counselling in higher education'. In S. Palmer and G. McMahon (eds) *Handbook of Counselling*. London: Routledge.

Jessica Benjamin (1990) *The Bonds of Love: Psychoanalysis, Feminism and the Problem of Domination*. London: Virago.

Alex Coren (1996) 'Brief therapy: base metal or pure gold?' *Psychodynamic Counselling* 2/1: 22–38.

Sheila Ernst (1987) 'Can a daughter be a woman?' In S. Ernst and M. Maguire (eds) *Living with the Sphinx: Papers from the Women's Therapy Centre*. London: Women's Press.

Ann Heyno (1996) 'Adhesive learning'. In *Culture and Psyche in Transition: A European Perspective on Student Psychological Health*. Papers from 25th Annual Training Event and Conference, Association for Student Counselling/Forum européen de l'orientation académique.

Isabel Menzies Lyth (1988) 'A report on a study of the nursing service of a general hospital' [1959]. In *Containing Anxiety in Institutions: Selected Essays by Isabel Menzies Lyth*. London: Free Association Books.

Margaret Tonnesmann (1993) 'The third area of experience in psychoanalysis'. In *Winnicott Studies* 8: 3–16.

Tara Weeramanthri (1997) 'Managing anxiety and the practitioner role'. In M. Lawrence and M. Maguire (eds) *Psychotherapy with Women: Feminist Perspectives*. London: Macmillan.

D.W. Winnicott (1991) 'The location of cultural experience' [1967]. In *Playing and Reality*. London: Routledge.

# 8    Issues of cultural difference in staff teams and client work

*Pat Grant*

Individual differences are a fact of life, even though many of us are uncomfortable with the reality of dealing with people who are different from us. There is a tendency to cope with this by imputing negative values to those who are not the same as we are. This has led to discrimination and the oppression of many minority groups who do not conform to certain cultural ideals. While it is true that most counsellors do not engage in overt discrimination and oppression, there is always the covert form, for example, failing to acknowledge cultural difference and judging others negatively when they fail to conform to the standards of the dominant culture. The reluctance to acknowledge racial and cultural differences is often due to the individual's fear of dealing with the meaning of difference (Green 1985) and possible coming face to face with their own oppressive and racist attitudes.

There are those who feel that less attention should be paid to differences between individuals and more to sameness. I disagree with that view, because an overemphasis on sameness is an excuse for not appreciating that while there are similarities between people, there are also many differences. Differences are wide ranging and include things such as race, ethnicity, culture, sexual orientation, gender, social class and physical disability. Our differences are what make us interesting, and this can be enriching to others if we give it opportunity. Counselling therefore demands a diverse approach, which 'means valuing differences and treating people in ways which bring out the best in them' (Ansari & Jackson 1995: 11).

In this chapter we shall be concentrating on cultural differences in staff teams and in counsellor/client work. The concept of culture will be explored and we shall examine some of the problems that can be caused by a negative approach to differences. We shall also be looking at ways in which we might benefit from differences and how to work effectively with differences.

## Culture

Culture is about the norms and values that are held by various groups in society. It is about similarities and differences in things such as language, style of expression, dress and a whole way of life that is passed from generation to generation. Culture allows us to separate one group of people from another on the basis of their distinctive pattern of behaviour. It is often taken for granted, but it should not be because 'it dictates our total existence from birth to death' (Vontress 1993: xii). Wherever we go we take our culture with us and it gives us a sense of belonging, particularly when we are with others of our own culture. The problem arises when we are with others from another culture who think their culture is superior to ours and that there is something wrong with us because we do not share their norms and values. There is a tendency for individuals to make judgements of others based on their own cultural norms and values. This is not surprising, because we can only work with what we know: however, if we are to relate effectively with those of another culture we will need to be more open and accepting of diversity.

## The problem of difference in staff teams

Counselling and psychotherapy have their own norms and values, passed down from one generation of students to the next: in other words, they have their own culture. I will go one step further by stating that each theoretical orientation in counselling/psychotherapy sets up its own culture, so there is a psychodynamic culture, a cognitive-behavioural culture and so on. It is possible that a staff team which subscribes to a particular culture could be very rejecting to staff who are not of their orientation. This behaviour may be seen in their response to colleagues who do not use the same theoretical language as they do and whose approach to case conceptualisation is different from theirs. This type of behaviour can leave some counsellors questioning their competence, simply because they do not approach cases in the same way as the rest of the staff team, who subscribe to a certain theoretical orientation.

Many staff teams which operate using a single orientation (e.g. psychodynamic) to counselling are, in theory, open to other approaches, even if they themselves do not use them. However, this apparent openness can sometimes be tested on occasions such as supervision, when a counsellor presents a case using an orientation that is different from that of the staff team's. Below is a mini case study to illustrate this point.

*Case study*

John Brown was appointed to work in a counselling team that was predominantly female. The team used a psychodynamic approach in their work with clients. John had a limited amount of experience in using the psychodynamic model, as he had admitted at interview, adding that his style of working was more person-centred. He was accepted into the team as they were keen to have a male counsellor.

After a month of working in the team John began to feel somewhat de-skilled. These feelings were more pronounced following group supervision sessions. He reported that he felt criticised for the way he approached working with clients. There often seemed to be a lot of questions about what he had not done, as well as interpretations that did not ring true to his experience of the clients. He felt that what he was doing with clients was not really appreciated or accepted.

John worked for three months in the above-mentioned team. During that period he was also receiving supervision from another supervisor for the work he did with clients in a different organisation. He reported that the supervisor in that organisation was accepting of his style of working and that he always left supervision feeling challenged, but never de-skilled. It was this latter experience, as well as feedback from clients, that enabled him to hold on to the fact that he was a good-enough counsellor.

Fernando (1988) wrote that therapists had to recognise the barriers to communication that may arise from cultural differences, for example a therapist's personal prejudice, linguistic problems, lack of knowledge of the cultures from which staff and clients come and so on. Staff teams are part of society and as such are not exempt from the prejudiced attitudes towards difference that can be seen in society. Recently, I was told of an incident in which the White secretary to a staff team would spray her office with air freshener after visits from Asian staff members. This member of staff justified her behaviour by saying that the Asian members of staff 'smelt'. (It is important to note that no other staff member had experienced their Asian colleagues in this way.) This secretary also had difficulty taking clear messages from Asian clients who phoned the service. It would seem that she had a prejudiced attitude towards Asians, and it was not surprising that she could not hear clearly what they were saying, because her prejudice blocked her hearing and robbed her of the patience she needed to listen to someone with a different accent.

Staff teams operate in institutions which exert control over how they function. Control comes in many forms, such as the number of sessions they are allowed to have with clients and the type of clients they can see. Many of these organisations lack sensitivity to cultural issues and in so doing exclude certain groups from the counselling service. For example, they may fail to provide access to the counselling service for disabled people. It is therefore left to staff teams either to collude with the institution or to take on the role of advocate to prevent such discriminatory practices.

Many staff teams do not reflect the range of differences that are present within the community they wish to serve. Keeping in mind that individuals tend to trust those who are more like them (Atkinson & Schien 1986), a team that does not reflect the community might have problems in attracting clients to the service and in keeping them for the duration of counselling. Another problem is that the staff team might lack knowledge of the various cultures within their catchment area. They might also lack the skills necessary to work with people of these cultures. Korman (1974) considered it unethical to provide counselling for people whose culture we do not understand and for whom we are not competent to provide a service. Sue et al. (1995) went further, stating that culturally unaware counsellors would be engaging in harmful and unethical cultural oppression.

## How to reduce prejudice and gain the benefits of individual differences in staff teams

In order to reduce prejudice, one must address the attitudes of team members. One might not be able to change team members' attitudes so that they have a more favourable approach to dealing with differences; however, one can provide situations that will facilitate these changes. The first step in this process is to help staff members to accept and respect themselves. It is impossible truly to respect and accept others who are different from us when we cannot demonstrate these attitudes to ourselves. Some counsellors belonging to the dominant culture are uncertain of their own racial and cultural identity. I believe that one of the reasons for this uncertainty is that they have never had cause to look beyond the fact that they are part of that dominant culture. I agree with the suggestion made by Rowe et al. (1995), that Whites might not experience a clear sense of racial identity in the same way as ethnic minority members of society do, because for Whites the salient factor that they must come to terms with is not their own difference, but rather that others are different. Counsellors in this position will need to engage in activities that will enable them to explore their own cultural identity before they can help clients to do this. The types of activities that might be useful are therapy and personal growth workshops where they have the time and space to explore who they are culturally. Spending time in an environment where they are in the minority could also be a useful way for such counsellors to appreciate *their* difference, as well as to acknowledge their sameness to others.

The second step involves getting to know fellow team members, finding out the ways in which they are similar to oneself and the ways in which they are different. Approaches such as these should help to reduce prejudice, which according to Allport (1954) is based on faulty and inflexible generalisation. Intercultural mixing is one of the keys to dispelling myths about other cultures. However, if this contact is be effective it needs to go beyond the superficial in order to allow stereotypes to be disconfirmed (Ponterotto & Pedersen 1993). One of the ways a staff team can promote intercultural mixing is for team members to share their work with others in the team, showing how they use themselves in the counselling process. In doing this team members will be able to demonstrate how their beliefs and attitudes influence their work.

Teams can also organise social events that promote intercultural mixing. One organisation arranges cultural evenings where staff take turns to give others in the team an insight into their culture. Aspects shared include food, art, literature and general information about the way of life of that culture. This sort of event can be very enlightening, not only for those listening but also for the presenter, to whom it can give a new appreciation of their own culture. This type of disclosure can also foster trust in staff teams.

I have highlighted the value of intercultural mixing in staff teams, but this can only occur if the team represents a range of cultures. Institutions should be encouraged to ensure that their teams cover a spectrum of differences and that, where possible, this reflects the differences in their local community.

The third step stems from the first two: having a basic acceptance of oneself and being clear about the differences and similarities that exist between oneself and other team members, one is then in a position to examine ways of making those differences work for the team. One of the ways this can work positively for the team is in the challenge that a team member of a different theoretical orientation can give. Someone who is not of the same theoretical orientation is less likely to take certain things for granted and so is more likely to ask questions. This can be useful, as it gives one the opportunity to question one's practice in a way one might otherwise not have done. Referrals might also be better facilitated, as we are more aware of the skills in the team and more respectful of what fellow team members can offer. Difference, then, could make a team more versatile and richer in what its members can offer clients as well as each other. Peer supervision is another way in which the team can benefit. Team members from other cultures can use supervision as a vehicle for teaching their peers how to work more effectively with clients from another culture. Below is an example of how peer supervision helped both the counsellor and the client.

*Case study*

Sandy was a White counsellor who was working with Brian, a Black male client. She had become very frustrated with Brian's 'resistive and challenging behaviour'. She could not understand why he was behaving in that way when she had done everything to make him feel comfortable. She suspected that Brian did not like her because she was White; however, she was worried about confronting him with this.

There was one Black counsellor on the staff team who had experience in working with Black clients, so Sandy thought she might use this person to provide her with supervision of this client. During the supervision it emerged that Sandy had a tendency to give in to Brian, and although Brian appeared to accept this he was always pushing the boundaries. Sandy was able to see how her fear of being seen as racist reduced her willingness to challenge Brian and how this in turn could have made the situation very unsafe for her client. The Black counsellor was also able to share with Sandy work from Sue and Sue (1990) which suggested that black clients sometimes expect their white counsellors to prove that they can be trusted, and that unless this proof is obtained they will fail to open up.

Sandy left the supervision having learnt something about herself as well as about how she might work more productively with Brian.

In order to provide an effective service to the culturally different there needs to be a team approach towards cultural diversity. This will ensure that good practices are shared and counsellors have the necessary training to give them confidence in their work with those who are different from themselves. The team approach might also include working with traditional healers where that is deemed appropriate, or taking on the role of advocate for culturally different clients.

## The problem of differences between counsellor and client

One of the major problems of differences between client and counsellor is often that of trust (Sue & Sue 1990). The exact reason for the lack of trust may vary, depending on the nature of the difference in question; however, fear of not being understood seems to exist in all forms. This is particularly so in the case of minority groups who have experienced oppression, directly or indirectly, by a dominant culture. Members of the dominant culture also experience distrust as they worry about whether or not they can trust minority group members not to treat them as oppressors. Both parties are therefore cautious in their relationship with each other.

Self-disclosure is necessary if counselling is to be effective; however, without trust the client will not feel free to engage in self-disclosure. The amount the client discloses is dependent upon the degree to which the counsellor and client perceive themselves as similar and acceptable to each other (Marsella & Pedersen 1981). Clients are often slow to disclose until they are fairly certain they can trust the counsellor – indeed, as was seen in the second case study, some clients might even push the counsellor into proving whether they are trustworthy. Counsellors may react poorly to proving that they can be trusted, because they often have little or no experience in doing this (Sue & Sue 1990). It therefore follows that when they are expected to do so by their culturally different clients many may react negatively, putting the blame on the client. This in turn would prevent the development of a good counselling relationship.

Cultural difference might also make communication difficult, even in situations where individuals supposedly speak the same language, for example English. In some cultures English words are used differently from the ways in which they are used by speakers from the majority culture, so if the counsellor is unaware of a client's usage of certain words or phrase, there could be communication problems. Counsellors will sometimes continue a conversation with a client thinking that they understand what is being said when in reality they do not, and at other times they will allow the client to continue speaking, even when they are unclear about what the client is saying. One of the main reasons they allow this is because they are afraid to admit they do not understand (possibly due to lack of trust) and they hope that as the conversation continues they will gain some understanding. The problem is that they rarely do catch on, and this just leads to more confusion and distrust within the relationship (Vontress 1981).

It is not unusual for counsellors to have a worldview different from that of their clients. One's worldview is the 'lens' through which the individual views the world (Ibrahim et al. 1994). 'Counsellors who hold a worldview different from that of their clients and are unaware of the basis for this difference are most likely to impute negative traits to clients' (Sue & Sue 1990:137). Consider the non-religious counsellor whose tendency is to conceptualise problems from a psychological perspective, working with a religious client who views their problem from a purely religious perspective; this situation can pose a block to a suitable working alliance. The case study below illustrates this point.

*Case study*

Mary was a West Indian woman who described herself as a 'born-again Pentecostal Christian'. She had recently lost two of her three children in a house fire and was referred for bereavement counselling by her family doctor. The counsellor she saw had no religious beliefs; however, she was greatly moved by Mary's story as she could see the psychological trauma this incident must have caused. Mary's perception of the situation was somewhat different from that of the counsellor: she saw it as the Devil's attack on her family. She was not going to let the Devil win by turning her back on God; instead, she was going to praise God through it all. Mary could not see what a counsellor could do, as it was prayer that would 'see her through'. The counsellor thought that Mary was in denial and the things she was saying were just a cover for her pain. Neither of these people was willing to accept the other's view, so they never really engaged. Maybe if the counsellor had accepted Mary's view as valid and looked at possible ways she could work with the church, the outcome might have been different.

Expectations that counsellors and clients have of each other and of the counselling process may be different if they are from different cultures. For example, some cultural groups would prefer a family approach to their problems rather than the individualistic one which is favoured by many Western counsellors. Many clients also expect behaviour different from that which the counsellors see themselves offering, and this could lead to a mismatch of expectations. According to Marsella et al. (1979), if a client comes from a background where they relate to authority in an autocratic way, then the tendency will be for them to do so in the therapeutic setting. They also expect the counsellor to be active, instructive and assertive. A number of writers (Fischer 1978; Baekeland & Lundwall 1975) have indicated that clients tend to drop out of therapy when their expectations differ from those of their therapists.

## Improving the counsellor/client relationship through the acknowledgement and appreciation of differences

In order to work effectively with the culturally different, counsellors will need to have certain characteristics. These include awareness of their own assumptions, values and biases, understanding of the worldview of their clients, and knowledge and skills in appropriate strategies needed to work with clients who are different from the counsellor (Sue & Sue 1990). Below is a further examination of each of these three characteristics.

## Awareness of assumptions, values and biases

The assumptions we make about others are often influenced by our own culture and most of the time we are not even aware that we are making them (Marsella & Pedersen 1981). In addition, the assumptions we make tend to be negative. If someone behaves in a way that differs from our cultural expectations, they are seen as odd/deviant. Counsellors will need to become more aware of the assumptions they make about their culturally different clients if they are to prevent these assumptions having a negative influence on their work. Green's advice to counsellors was to 'confront their own biases when dealing with any culturally diverse group' (1985: 390). This is a necessary prerequisite for working with differences, as our biases influence our perception of normal and abnormal. It is not unusual for the Black family to be branded as pathological by White counsellors and others whose view of normality is restricted by their culture (Fernando 1988; Littlewood & Lipsedge 1981). In order to enjoy a positive working relationship with their clients, counsellors need to see strengths in different cultures and be less quick to pathologise; maybe then fewer ethnic minority group members would be labelled with a psychiatric diagnosis. In many ethnic minority cultures the extended family, flexibility in family roles, religion and various social networks can be sources of strength that can be mobilised to help the client. One of the dangers of pathologising is that we fail to see these strengths and so we cannot use them to help the clients. Let us return to Mary, who was mentioned earlier: one of the strengths of West Indian culture is religious belief. Maybe if the counsellor had accepted Mary's belief in the existence of the Devil and the power that could be gained through praising God, she would have been able to engage Mary in counselling. It is also possible that she could have liaised with the church in her work with Mary, thus utilising the vast support network it offers.

Each cultural group has its own preferred way of receiving help and counsellors need to find out what this is in order to be of help. For many groups the counselling room might not be the ideal setting; indeed, self-help groups and religious groups might be more acceptable. Atkinson, Thompson and Grant (1993) found that in working with certain cultural groups out-of-office sites such as the client's home, churches and voluntary organisations may be more therapeutic and effective. They also went on to say that alternative roles such as that of change agent or advocate may be more useful. Counsellors will therefore have to learn how to work in these ways if they want to meet the needs of their clients. This approach will, of course, challenge the value counsellors place on the privacy of their counselling room.

### Understanding the worldview of the client

It is impossible adequately to address the needs of clients unless one has some idea about how these clients view their individual, group and cultural identity. The counsellor will also need to know about the values and beliefs that influence the client's view of the world. This will, for example, influence how the client sees counselling and their willingness to engage in it. Often frustration and anxiety in counselling are due to lack of understanding (Ibrahim 1985). Counsellors can increase their understanding of the client by exploring these and other issues during the counselling process. There is, however, information about the culture that counsellors could find out if they did their homework prior to seeing the client. As was mentioned earlier, counsellors have a responsibility to inform themselves about the cultures of predominant groups of people living in the area in which they work.

There are many factors such as oppression and discrimination which can influence a group's identity and without an understanding of these the counsellor may not be as helpful as they might otherwise have been. Clients who have experienced discrimination, oppression, powerlessness, exclusion and poverty will have a different view of the world from that of the counsellor, whose experience might be one of privilege. Counsellors therefore need to demonstrate their understanding of the client's position by the respect they give to the client's view of the world and also by the validity they attach to that view. Attention must also be paid to the external conditions that affect the lives of our culturally different clients. It may not be helpful to move directly into deeper intrapsychic concerns when clients are still stuck with external issues that are important to them. It we want to engage and keep our culturally different clients then we must deal with what is important for them. This is not to imply that all the problems of the culturally different revolve around external factors or being different, simply that these must be acknowledged.

Counsellors who are knowledgeable about the socio-political system and the impact of this on the culturally different are more able to 'quickly attune to what may be issues for their client' (Turner 1991: 407). They are also more likely to be direct in their dealings with their clients and are more able to link counselling to the current experiences of their culturally different clients. In doing this they provide a service that is culturally sensitive. Clients engage better and disclose more when counsellors are culturally sensitive and responsive basically because they are perceived as more credible (Atkinson, Morten & Sue 1993b).

## Developing appropriate strategies for working with the culturally different

Counsellors wishing to work with the culturally different will need to develop a wide range of skills. It will not be enough to cling to any one orientation and the skills associated with it, as many culturally different clients may not be able to work in that way and so will not be able to use the counselling on offer. A number of reports (e.g. Marsella et al. 1979; Sue 1981) indicate that clients from certain cultural groups prefer their counsellors to be more active, instructive, assertive and directive. This being the case, many counsellors would need to extend their range of skills to incorporate such approaches when working with these clients. This is not to suggest that counsellors should not have a preferred way of working with clients, but rather that, in addition, they should have knowledge and skills related to other approaches that might be user-friendly to their culturally different clients. For many people the idea of counselling is anxiety provoking and they enter counselling feeling very vulnerable. They need the warmth of the counsellor if they are to become open and share their concerns. The expression of warmth is culturally determined so it can be a challenge for counsellors as they seek to find ways of expressing warmth that are comfortable for both them and their clients.

In our society there is a lot of pressure placed on those who are different to conform to what the dominant culture deems acceptable. Over time, the culturally different have developed a range of strategies for dealing with the pressure, prejudice and discrimination. Some of the strategies they develop consciously, others unconsciously. One of the tasks of counsellors is to help clients to become conscious of all the strategies they use and to explore other available strategies. Having examined all the strategies available to them, clients can then make a conscious choice about the ones they use. Throughout all this the counsellor's approach will be non-judgemental and free from pressure on the client to conform. This atmosphere is conducive to self-acceptance and openness on the part of the client.

Counsellors interested in establishing a good counselling relationship with their culturally different clients would benefit from gaining some insight into how different groups develop their cultural identity. According to Sue and Sue (1990), there is evidence to suggest that the cultural identity of clients influences their reaction to the counselling, the counsellor and the counselling process. Let us take a client who is at the 'Resistance and Immersion' stage (Atkinson, Morten & Sue 1993b). This person is often anti-establishment, tends to view counselling services and counsellors as part of the 'oppressive establishment' and is therefore unwilling to engage with them. Sue and Sue (1990) also go on to suggest that the high dropout rate of the culturally different from counselling could be linked to failure to accurately assess their cultural identity.

There are a variety of cultural identity models available, including Atkinson, Morten and Sue (1993a) and Helms (1995). These models provide one with a conceptual framework for understanding how different groups develop their cultural identity. They help us to discover the types of needs that clients may present at different stages of their development and also the demands they might make on the counsellor. An appreciation of these factors will give counsellors insight into how they might intervene. For example, an Asian student was referred to an Asian counsellor in the university. The student was very reluctant to work to work with an Asian counsellor and demonstrated this in a number of ways. The counsellor, being familiar with racial/cultural identity models, was able to assess what stage of development the client was at and make appropriate interventions. The counsellor did not take the client's behaviour 'personally', but rather saw it as an indication of where that client was in her cultural development. The example of Sandy and Brian given earlier could also be looked at from a cultural identity perspective. It would seem that Brian was at a stage in his development where he needed to challenge Sandy and have her prove that she could be trusted (Atkinson, Morten & Sue 1993b).

An understanding of cultural identity development is not only useful in the assessment of clients; it is also helpful in assisting counsellors to assess their own cultural identity. This is as important as the former because the stage of development that the counsellor is at will influence how they work with clients. For example, let us assume that the Asian counsellor mentioned earlier was at a stage in her cultural development where she was opposed to the dominant culture but proud of her own and very committed to spending time with people of her culture. This counsellor could therefore be rather hostile to the Asian client who did not want to work with her, which would make it impossible to establish any sort of working relationship.

## Conclusion

Working with people who are different from us can give rise to uncomfortable feelings, because many of us still have the negative values about difference that we acquired while growing up. While these values might have been acquired years ago via such sources as the media and our families, they still affect our lives consciously and unconsciously. One of the effects of that negative attitude to difference is in the way that many of us pressure those who are different to conform to the norms of the dominant culture. This type of pressure and the prejudice that underlies it could make it difficult to establish a working alliance with those who are different from us. On the other hand, if we value difference and adopt a diverse approach we will be able to bring out the best in ourselves and in others. 'Diversity challenges the counselling profession to continuous growth, fluidity and evolution, it defies stagnation' (Grieger & Ponterotto 1995: 372). In working with diversity, counsellors have the opportunity to extend their roles and to work in different ways. They also have a chance to move out of their offices and into the community to meet and work with clients where they are and where they feel comfortable. This sort of venture is quite daunting for some but it offers the possibility for some profitable work between counsellors and clients. It also provides the staff team with the sort of energy and vibrancy that defies stagnation.

# References

Allport, G. (1954) *The Nature of Prejudice*. Cambridge, Mass.: Addison-Wesley

Ansari, K. and Jackson, J. (1995) *Managing Culture: Diversity at Work*. London: Kogan Page

Atkinson, D. and Schien, S. (1986) 'Similarity in counselling', *The Counselling Psychologist* 4, pp. 319–354

Atkinson, D., Morten, G. and Sue, D., eds (1993a) *Counseling American Minorities: a Cross-cultural Perspective*, 4th edition. Dubuque, IA: William Brown

Atkinson, D., Morten, G. and Sue, D. (1993b) 'A minority identity development model' [1989], in Atkinson, D., Morten, G. and Sue, D. (eds) *Counseling American Minorities: A Cross-cultural Perspective*. Dubuque, IA: William Brown, pp. 35–52

Atkinson, D., Thompson, C. and Grant, S. (1993) 'A three dimensional model for counseling racial/ethnic minorities', *The Counseling Psychologist* 21, pp. 257–277

Baekeland, F. and Lundwall, L. (1975) 'Dropping out of treatment: A critical review', *Psychological Bulletin*, 82, pp. 738–783

Fernando, S. (1988) *Race and Culture in Psychiatry*. London: Croom Helm

Fischer, J. (1978) *Effective Casework Practice: An Eclectic Approach*. New York: McGraw-Hill

Green, B. (1985) 'Consideration in the treatment of black patients by white therapists', *Psychotherapy* 22(2) pp. 389–393

Grieger, I. and Ponterotto, J. (1995) 'A framework for assessment in multicultural counseling', in Ponterotto, J., Casas, M., Suzuki, L. and Alexander, C. (eds) *Handbook of Multicultural Counseling*. London: Sage, pp. 357–374

Helms, J. (1995) 'An update of Helms's white and people of color identity model', in Ponterotto, J., Casas, M., Suzuki, L and Alexander, C. (eds) *Handbook of Multicultural Counseling*. London: Sage, pp. 181–198

Ibrahim, F. (1985) 'Effective cross-cultural counseling and psychotherapy: A framework', *The Counseling Psychologist* 13, pp. 625–636

Ibrahim, F., Ohrishi, H., Wilson, R. (1994) 'Career assessment in a culturally diverse society', *Journal of Career Assessment* 2, pp. 276–288

Korman, M. (1974) 'National conference on levels and patterns of professional training in psychology: Major themes', *American Psychologist* 29, pp. 301–313

Littlewood, R. and Lipsedge, M. (1981) 'Acute psychotic reaction in Caribbean-born patients', *Psychological Medicine* 11, pp. 303–318

Marsella, A. and Pedersen, P. (1981) *Cross-cultural Counselling and Psychotherapy*. New York: Pergamon

Marsella, A., Tharp, R. and Ciborowski, T., eds (1979) *Perspectives in Cross-cultural Psychology*. New York: Academic Press

Ponterotto, J. and Pedersen, P., eds (1993) *Preventing Prejudice: A Guide for Counsellors and Educators*. London: Sage

Rowe, W., Behrens, J. and Leach, M. (1995) 'Racial ethnic identity and racial consciousness: looking back and looking forward', in Ponterotto, J., Casas, M., Suzuki, L. and Alexander, C. (eds) *Handbook of Multicultural Counseling*. London: Sage, pp. 218–235

Sue, D. (1981) 'Evaluating process variables in cross-cultural counseling and psychotherapy', in Marsella, A. and Pedersen, P. (ed) *Cross Cultural Counseling and Psychotherapy*. New York: Pergamon, pp. 181–184

Sue, D. and Sue, D. (1990) *Counseling the Culturally Different: Theory and Practice*. New York: Wiley

Sue, D., Arredondo, P. and McDavis, R. (1995) 'Multicultural counseling competencies and standard: A call to the profession', in Ponterotto, J., Casas, M., Suzuki, L. and Alexander, C. (eds) *Handbook of Multicultural Counseling*. London: Sage, pp. 624–640

Turner, J. (1991) 'Migrants and their therapist: A trans-context approach', *Family Process* 30, pp. 407–419

Vontress, C. (1981) 'Racial and ethnic barriers in counseling', in Pedersen, P., Dragus, J., Lonner, N. and Trimble, J. (eds) *Counseling Across Cultures*. Honolulu: University of Hawaii Press, pp. 87–107

Vontress, C. (1993) 'Foreword', in Ponterotto, J. and Pedersen, P. (eds) *Preventing Prejudice: A Guide for Counselors and Educators*. London: Sage, pp. xi–xiii

# 9  Working directly with political, social and cultural material in the therapy session

*Andrew Samuels*

The roots of this chapter actually lie in a number of recent political developments with which I have been closely involved. I have carried out a number of consultations with politicians in Britain and the United States designed to explore how useful and effective perspectives derived from psychotherapy might be in the formation of policy and in new thinking about the political process. It is difficult to present psychotherapeutic thinking about politics so that mainline politicians – for example, a Democratic senator or a Labour Party committee – will take it seriously. I have found that issues of gender and sexuality are particularly effective in this regard. Partly this is due to the perennial fascination and excitement carried by such topics. Partly it is due to the feminist politicization of such issues over the past thirty years, which has gradually led to their presence on the agenda of mainstream politics. Partly it is because gender is itself a hybrid notion from a political point of view. On one level, in the social world of lived experience, gender and sexuality are everyday realities, suffused with experiences of power, powerlessness, vulnerability and misunderstanding. Gender has its own socio-economic dimensions and set of electoral significances. But, on another level, gender is also an exceedingly private business as part of a story that people tell themselves and have told to them in attempts to produce, create or discover identities and relationships with others. Gender and sexuality are therefore liminal, sitting on the threshold between internal and external worlds, contributing to and partaking of both.

I have also been involved in the formation of three organizations whose objectives are relevant to the content of this chapter. Psychotherapists and Counsellors for Social Responsibility is a professional organization intended to facilitate the desire of many psychotherapists, analysts and counsellors to intervene as professionals in social and political matters making appropriate use of their knowledge and, it must be admitted, whatever cultural authority they possess. The second organization is a psychotherapy-based think-tank, Antidote. Here, the strategy has been to limit the numbers of mental health professionals involved so as to reduce the chances of psychotherapy reductionism and foster multidisciplinary work in the social policy field. Antidote has undertaken research work in connection with psychological attitudes to money and economic issues generally, and is also involved in work in the area of 'emotional literacy', but expanding the usual remit from personal relationships and family matters to include issues in the public domain. The third organization is a broad front based at St James's Church in London. The St James's Alliance consists of individuals from diverse fields such as politics, economics, ethics, religion, non-governmental organizations, the media and psycho-therapy. It attempts to incorporate ethical, spiritual and psychological concerns into the British political agenda and to facilitate a dialogue between non-governmental organizations, single-issue groups and progres-sive political organizations. It is an experiment in gathering in political energy that is split up and dissipated under current arrangements.

It will be thought that psychotherapists and analysts such as myself are making these moves from on-high and from a detached position, careless of the political issues affecting our own profession. However, all three organizations have been active in and profoundly affected by the acrimonious yet relatively successful campaign waged by elements of the psychotherapy profession to end discrimination against lesbians and gay men as candidates for training in psychoanalytic psychotherapy and psychoanalysis. When psychotherapists engage in politics they need to do so with a degree of consciousness of the appalling mess in which their own professional politics are usually to be found, as well as irony or even self-mockery as regards the counter-intuitive and slightly mad content of much of what they have to say.

## What shall we do about politics?

In this chapter I explore how the practice of psychotherapy might be politicized so that therapists and analysts who seek to work with the whole person, including the social and political dimensions of the experiences of their clients, may do so with greater confidence and clarity. I believe this detailed work has not really been done yet. I shall not be focusing much on the external and internal political dynamics of the therapy encounter itself and hardly at all on the aforementioned politics of the profession, though these both remain concerns of mine. Therapy is embedded in politics and culture; therapy has its own politics and culture. These are pretty obvious points by now. Instead, I intend to present some ideas about the relationship of therapy practice to politics. Although these ideas derive from work with individuals, they may be even more pertinent and useful in group analysis and psychotherapy. The group matrix may facilitate the politicization of the practice of therapy rather well (see Brown & Zinkin 1994, *passim*).

By 'politics' I mean the concerted arrangements and struggles within an institution, or in a single society, or between the countries of the world for the organization and distribution of power, especially economic power. Economic and political power includes control of processes of information and representation to serve the interests of the powerful as well as the use of physical force and possession of vital resources such as land, food, water or oil.

On a more personal level, there is a second kind of politics. Here, political power reflects struggles over agency, meaning the ability to choose freely whether to act and what action to take in a given situation. This is often a feeling-level politics, a politics of subjectivity, a politics to which feminism introduced us.

But politics also refers to a crucial interplay between these two dimensions, between the public and the personal dimensions of power. There are connections between economic power and power as expressed on the domestic, private level. Power is a process or network as much as a stable factor. This version of political power is experienced psychologically: in family organization, gender and race relations, and in religious and artistic assumptions as they affect the lives of individuals.

Where the public and the private, the political and the personal, intersect, I think there is a special role for analysis and psychotherapy in relation to political change and transformation. The tragicomic crisis of our *fin de siècle* civilization incites us to challenge the boundaries that are conventionally accepted as existing between the external world and the internal world, between life and reflection, between extroversion and introversion, between doing and being, between politics and psychology, between the political development of the person and the psychological development of the person, between the fantasies of the political world and the politics of the fantasy world. Subjectivity and intersubjectivity have some political roots; they are not as 'internal' as they seem.

There is little point in working on the orientation of psychotherapy to the world of politics if its own basic theories and practices remained completely unaltered. I support the continuing practice of therapy and analysis with individuals and small groups. This is because I do not agree that analysis and therapy inevitably syphon off rage that might more constructively be deployed in relation to social injustices. In fact, I think that it is the reverse that often happens: experiences in therapy act to fine down generalized rage into a more constructive form, hence rendering emotion more accessible for social action. Even when this is not what happens, the potential remains for a move from private therapy to public action – and I propose to discuss that potential in this chapter.[1]

The idea is to develop a portrayal of the clinical setting as a bridge between psychology or psychotherapy and politics, rather than as the source of an isolation from politics. Critics of the clinical project of depth psychology (e.g. Hillman & Ventura 1992) have noted the isolation – and this is not a totally wrong observation. But I want us also to see the potential links and to create a truly radical revisioning of clinical work, not a simplistic huffing and puffing aimed at its elimination.

One of the most potent criticisms of therapy and analysis is that the client is encouraged or even required to turn away from external concerns – for example, political commitments – and focus exclusively on the 'inner world'. This, it is argued, makes any statement about therapy engaging the whole person an absolute nonsense.[2] Textbooks of therapy and analysis accentuate the introspection by making it clear that exploration of outer world issues is simply not done in 'proper' therapy and analysis.

Humanistic psychotherapy in its early days seemed to have this kind of vision of therapy in mind but, since the growth of a desire to integrate psychoanalytic thinking, humanistic psychotherapists seem to have adopted a psychoanalytic professional ego-ideal or even super-ego. When I made this point at the 1997 Professional Conference of the United Kingdom Council for Psychotherapy, the numerous humanistic psychotherapists present clearly knew what I was talking about (Samuels 1998).

Over a period of time, I sensed that this professional consensus was collapsing and that therapists and analysts were indeed beginning to pay more attention to what could be called the political development of their clients (see pp. 134–7). In my own practice I noticed that many clients seemed to be introducing political themes more often than they had before. Talking to colleagues confirmed that this was also going on in their work, so it was not all due to suggestion on my part. We tended to put it down to the fact that, since the mid-1980s, the pace of political change in the world appeared to have quickened. At times, I still felt that the usual formulation – that such material needs to be understood as symbolic of what is going on in the client – worked pretty well. At other times it turned out that the client had a need to talk about some public issue, maybe to work out what their true feelings and opinions were. But the client might also have learned that you're not supposed to do that in therapy or analysis. For example, during the Gulf War there were certainly some clients who used war imagery to tell me something about their inner state. Yet there were others who were hiding a profound need to talk about the Gulf War behind the flow of regular, ordinary clinical material.

I decided that what was needed was a large-scale investigation, by means of a questionnaire, to see if analysts and therapists were experiencing something similar in significant numbers. I therefore obtained the co-operation of 14 professional organizations with differing theoretical orientations in 7 different countries and sent out 2,000 survey forms. I got a return rate of almost exactly one-third (quite high for a cold-calling survey on which the respondents had to spend some time and write fairly lengthy and thoughtful answers).

In the survey, I asked which themes of a list of fifteen possibles were the most frequently introduced by clients. This produced a worldwide league table as follows: (1) gender issues for women, (2) economic issues (e.g. distribution of wealth, poverty, inflation), (3) violence in society, (4=) national politics, and gender issues for men, (4=) racial or ethnic issues, (6) international politics. ·

There were some striking departures from the order. For instance, the German analysts placed 'the environment' at the top of the list as the most frequently introduced issue whilst for the British psychoanalysts economic issues came in seventh. This enables us to make all kinds of speculations about whether there is or is not something like a 'national psyche' or 'collective consciousness' – at least as evidenced in the political themes the clients of therapists and analysts bring to their sessions.

I asked the participants how they reacted to, handled or interpreted the material. 78 per cent of the respondents mentioned that they understood the material as referring in some sense to reality. For many, this was in conjunction with a symbolic interpretation or an exploration of why the client was interested in that particular theme at that particular moment. The replies – thoughtful and extensive – showed considerable struggle by the respondents as they endeavoured to mark out their positions.

I went on to ask if the respondent 'discussed' politics with his or her clients. Of course, I realized the explosive nature of the question and deliberately did not define what might be covered by the word 'discuss'. Worldwide, 56 per cent said they did discuss politics and 44 per cent that they did not. American Jungian analysts do the most discussing (72 per cent) and British psychoanalysts the least (33 per cent). However, it is interesting to note that the implication of the one third 'yes' of the British psychoanalysts is that 43 of them admit to discussing politics with clients (one-third of the 129 respondents).

I asked the respondents the obvious question: 'Have you ever been/are you politically active?' 67 per cent said they had been politically active at some time – a figure which, unsurprisingly, dropped to 33 per cent at the present time. My intuitive impression, just from talking to colleagues, that a good many of them had been politically active at some time was borne out. The stereotype of a profession composed of introspective, introverted, self-indulgent types was challenged.

So what might it all mean? In the most down-to-earth terms, it could mean that if a person is contemplating analysis or therapy, and if that person is interested in politics (however defined), it would be as well to explore with a potential therapist or analyst what they are likely to do if one brings political material to the consulting room. For the profession is clearly divided about it. Even if everyone who did not return the survey forms abhors politics in the consulting room, there is still a significant minority of practitioners who do not. This other, hitherto unknown group of clinicians sees that involvement in and concern for the world is part of growing up, of individuation, and maybe even part of mental health. The split in the therapy profession is at its most destructive when it is between the public, apolitical, hyperclinical face of the profession – something that has quite rightly been criticized – and a much more politically aware, private face of the profession. Many therapists and analysts seem all too aware that they are citizens too, that they have political histories themselves, that they too struggle to find the balance between inner-looking and outer-looking attitudes. As a British psychoanalyst put it when replying to the questionnaire:

> We are political animals. Everything we are and do takes place within a political framework. It is impossible to divorce this from the inner world of either our patients or ourselves.

The survey on political material brought to the clinical setting was not a scientific instrument, nor even a conventional social scientific instrument. Nevertheless, several eminent social scientists have kindly commented that my methodology not only resembles certain cutting-edge practices in social science ('naturalistic research') and was appropriate to my project. The survey has been published in a leading sociology journal (Samuels 1994). Hence I hope that discussion of the survey will not only focus on issues of methodology, thereby distracting us from my overall thesis, which is that as psychoanalysis and psychotherapy move into the next century, the range of material suitable for clinical investigation should expand to include political themes and issues. If this were to happen, then we would move one small step nearer to realizing the ideal of an analysis of the whole person. Moreover – and maybe this is the crucial thing – therapists and analysts would also move one small step towards realizing the century-old project of depth psychology to shed light on what Freud referred to as 'the riddles of the world'. (See Samuels 1993: 209–266 for a fuller account of the survey.)

## Politicizing therapy practice

When attempting to link psychoanalysis or psychotherapy with political and social issues, we need to establish a two-way street. In one direction travel men and women of the psyche, bringing what they know of human psychology to bear on the crucial political and social issues of the day, such as leadership, the market economy, nationalism, racial prejudice and environmentalism. Going the other way down this street, we try to get at the hidden politics of personal life as broadly conceived and understood: the politics of early experience in the family, gender politics, and the politics of internal imagery, usually regarded as private. The dynamic that feminism worked upon between the personal and the political is also a dynamic between the psychological and the social. It is so complicated that to reduce it in either one direction (all psyche) or the other direction (all sociopolitical), or to assert a banal, holistic synthesis that denies difference between these realms is massively unsatisfactory. There is a very complicated interplay, and this chapter trades off the energy in that interplay. One hope is to develop a new, hybrid language of psychology and politics that will help us to contest conventional notions of what 'politics' is and what 'the political' might be. The aspirations of so many disparate groups of people worldwide – environmentalists, human rights activists, liberation theologians, feminists, pacifists and peacemakers, ethnopoliticians – for a reinvented and resacralized politics would gain the support of the psychological and psychotherapy communities.

It is worthwhile focusing on therapy and on clinical work for two main reasons. First, because the results of the survey show that this is a hot issue for practitioners just now. Second, because exploring the politicization of practice might help to answer the awkward question: why has the political world not shown up for its first session with the therapists who are so keen to treat it? Freud, Jung and the great humanistic pioneers like Maslow and Rogers truly wanted to engage with the institutions and problematics of society. But they, and even more their followers, did this in such an on-high, experience-distant, mechanical fashion, with the secret agenda of proving their own theories correct, that the world has been, quite rightly, suspicious. Objecting to psychological reductionism in relation to political and social is reasonable – not resistance. But what if clinical experience were factored in? At the very least, there would be a rhetorical utility. For, without their connection to the clinic, to therapy, why should anyone in the world of politics listen to the psychotherapeutic people at all? What do we have to offer it if doesn't include something from our therapy work? Therapy is certainly not all that we have to offer, but it is the base.

The professional stakes are very high. In certain sectors of humanistic and transpersonal psychology clinical work is becoming more overtly politicized so that the whole client may be worked with. But this is still very much a minority view in the psychodynamic and psychoanalytic sectors of psychotherapy. Politically speaking, most clinical practice constitutes virgin territory. The stakes are so high because what people like me are trying to do is to change the nature of the field, change the nature of the profession – that which we profess, believe and do. As the survey showed, this attempt is part of a worldwide movement in which the general tendency is to extend the nature of the psychotherapy field so as to embrace the social and political dimensions of experience.

If we do want to treat the whole person, as some of us do, then we have to find detailed ways of making sure that the social and political dimensions of experience are included in the therapy process regularly, reliably, and as a matter of course. We must try to achieve a situation in which the work is political always already. Not unusually, not exceptionally, not only when it is done by mavericks, but when it is done in an everyday way by Everytherapist.

The detailed work is not easy to do. About seven years ago a remarkable book appeared entitled *Psychoanalysis and the Nuclear Threat: Clinical and Theoretical Studies* (Levine et al. 1988). All the editors and all the contributors were the most *echt*, kosher psychoanalysts one could find – they were all, in fact, members of the American Psychoanalytic Association. The following passage appears in the editorial introduction:

> In the best of circumstances analysts may assume that considerations of politics are irrelevant to the analytic space. We raise the possibility here that the potential of nuclear weapons for destroying the world intrudes into the safety of that space. We no longer live in the best of circumstances. Thus, the construct of a socially, culturally, and politically neutral analytic setting may be a fantasy, one that embodies the wish that the outside can be ignored, denied, or wished away.

In a basically favourable review of this book, the psychoanalyst and social critic Alexander Gralnick stated:

> Unfortunately, few of the contributors to the theoretical part of the book deal with the many important assumptions and unsettled issues in psychoanalytic thought and clinical practice that the editors hoped consideration of the nuclear threat would prompt them to discuss . . . Though bound by traditional concepts, some authors seemed to recognize that psychoanalysts may not be as neutral as they

believe themselves to be . . . These psychoanalysts are plagued by their own resistances and anxieties about the further changes they face and how creative they dare be; they are naturally limited by being at *the earliest stages* of changes we all face, and, like the rest of us, are *handicapped by lack of a needed new language*.

(1990: 68; emphases added)

I, too, am at the earliest stages of this project, and I, too, am handicapped by the lack of a much-needed new language. These thoughts and speculations are my best shot.

I shall eventually be discussing and proposing the politicization of therapy practice under the following headings:

1   The therapeutic value of political discussion in the session;
2   Exploring the political myth of the person in therapy;
3   The hidden politics of internal, private imagery;
4   Citizen-as-therapist – a therapeutic model for political engagement;
5   Working out a socialized, transpersonal psychology of community.

However, as the project has developed, I have found it useful at the outset to attempt to deal with, or at least discuss, the objections to what is being proposed. In this way, readers are alerted to my own awareness of the radical and often risky nature of these ideas. Moreover, dealing first with the objections resembles good psychoanalytic technique whereby resistance is analysed before content. Of course, the objections are not only resistance and I am convinced that an ongoing engagement with objections (and objectors) to the politicization of therapy practice is enhancing for all sides in the debate.

The first objection is that removing the focus of the clinical enterprise away from the internal world and onto the political world constitutes bad clinical practice. The reply to that objection can be equally assertive. Foreclosure on politics, the privileging and valorizing of the internal over the external, may, as we stagger towards the end of the century, itself constitute bad clinical practice. From today's perspective, maybe I *do* want or need to do some bad practice as I change my practice. Those who do not or cannot change their practices may, from tomorrow's point of view, be the ones guilty of bad practice. What is or is not 'on' in clinical technique has evolved strikingly over the psychoanalytic century. These matters are *not* definitively settled.

The second objection concerns the problem of suggestion and undue influence on the part of the therapist. This is a sensitive issue these days, given the moral panic surrounding psychotherapy stemming from the notion of false memory syndrome. Is there a risk that a politicized therapy practitioner will foist his or her own political ideas, principles, and values onto the vulnerable, open-to-suggestion client? Would not that be a shattering objection to the politicization of therapy? In reply, I would ask if we are really supposed to believe that a practitioner who sticks to the way he or she was trained and keeps the political out of the consulting room is thereby devoid of the sin of ever suggesting anything to the client. Many studies show that an enormous amount of influencing by the therapist of the client goes on, and in fact may be essential for some kind of psychological movement to happen. At times, even Freud equates transference and suggestion, making a defensive point which also serves me well: you cannot suggest something into somebody unless they are ready for it, unless it 'tallies' with what is already alive in them. I would use Freud against the objection. Suggestion is going on already. There is no reason to suppose that a politicized practitioner would necessarily be intruding his or her own values more than somebody whose interest was in object relations, sexuality, aggression, spirituality or the soul.

Of course, there is always a risk of discipleship in the psychotherapy situation as those who have had training therapy know. But I feel confident in saying that there is today a huge amount of uncritically accepted suggestion in clinical practice and that, from a certain point of view, the more 'bounded', 'contained' and 'disciplined' the behaviour of the practitioner, the more suggestion is taking place in his or her practice. I think this is inevitable. The technical rules of analysis are not politically or culturally neutral; they do more than 'facilitate' the unfolding of the self. They have themselves cultured depth psychology in a permanent way, and they have themselves done it to a certain extent by suggestion. On the basis of the replies received to the questionnaire on political material that is brought to the consulting room, it is clear that a good deal of rule breaking goes on in ordinary therapy and analysis – probably much more than is revealed in supervision, wherein words like 'discussion' are dirty words. If psychotherapists and analysts are already discussing politics with the client, then it is clear that the hygienic sealing of the consulting room from politics is a virginal fantasy on the part of practitioners.

The third objection concerns what is to be done when the therapist is confronted with somebody with political views he or she finds repulsive. Discussing my ideas at a meeting of the British Association of Psychotherapists, I was once asked: 'What would happen if Hitler came into your consulting room?' Well, psychodynamically speaking, I think I have seen quite a few Hitler-types in my consulting room already. Although this point cannot settle the very real worries that working with somebody whose views you find repulsive creates, surely we can agree that, from time to time, every practitioner will meet a version of this problem. Moreover, politics is not the only source of repulsion.

A fourth objection concerns the alleged élitism of what I am proposing. Do I have some kind of fantasy that we are going to send a well-analysed vanguard of the psychopolitical revolution out into the world? Of course I have had that fantasy from time to time but, in a more moderate vein, and in terms of developing an argument about changing the field, I do not for one minute think that a person who has had psychological analysis or therapy is in some kind of élite vanguard. However, as indicated, I do recognize that there is some strength in this objection, and I try to stay conscious of the problem.

The fifth objection is extremely subtle and hence difficult to deal with. This objector claims that he or she is carrying out a political therapy practice already. Sometimes I feel that this is undoubtedly the case. At other times, when I am told that the mere practice of therapy, or even just the making of interpretations, are political acts, I must demur. Similarly, when it is blandly observed that all of inner life obviously involves the outer world, including politics, and there's no point in going on about it, I feel I need to know about the fate of the outer world in therapy done by such an objector. I think it is a sign of the times that many practitioners do not want to admit to working oblivious to the world of politics. The rules of the game are changing. And, as the survey shows, it is clear that many people are trying to work in a more politically attuned way. But the mere recognition that inner and outer are connected cannot constitute a politicization of practice. This is a difficult objection to engage with, being told that politicizing practice is all old hat and that everyone is doing it. It injures the narcissism of the pioneer!

A sixth objection concerns the scope and timing of political work in therapy. I am often asked if these ideas are applicable to every client. Of course, they are not. There is a further question in connection with timing and it is certainly important to wait and see where the client is headed. This is easy to say but I think there may be a smear in the way this objection is sometimes posed, in that the not-so-secret intent is to characterize political work as inappropriate and likely to be done in a clumsy way. Sometimes, a politicized therapist will mistime or misplace his or her interventions. But therapists often take ideas derived from object relations or archetypal theory or psychosexuality and make use of them in situations where these ideas turn out to be woefully inappropriate and irrelevant. It happens all the time and it is not meant as damaging to the client. Somehow 'politics' is singled out as more likely to lead to such an abuse of the client.

While there is little doubt that political action outside the therapy entered into by a client can be defensive or resistant, this is surely not always the case. Sometimes, when working with politically active clients, there has come a move from within the client to withdraw from politics for a while – and this is, of course, respected. Nevertheless, we might perhaps question the psychoanalytic (or maybe the bourgeois) depreciation of action in general and political action in particular. Political action is psychologically valid, positive and creative. Not to act would sometimes constitute a special form of repression – a repression supported by the institutions of therapy and analysis themselves.

A seventh objection shows the professional politics of the psycho-analytic world at their worst. Consider this reply written by a senior British psychoanalyst to the questionnaire that asked him how he relates to, deals with and manages overtly political material brought to the clinical situation. This is a highly intelligent and articulate man, but attend carefully to the didactic way in which the party line is delivered:

> Although I believe that the insights of psychoanalysis . . . are highly relevant to political and social structure, and am (broadly speaking) committed to a leftish political set of beliefs, most of the questions you ask seem to me to be based on a very profound misunderstanding of the nature of psychoanalytic treatment, in which the analyst's listening to the patient takes place within the framework of the analyst's theory of transference: everything the patient says has mean-ing in other contexts and much of what he reports and says will be more or less true and relevant in such contexts, but in the context of the psychoanalytical session, the meaning which it is the analyst's job to apprehend is that concerned with what the patient is communicating to the analyst at that moment about the state of his internal fantasy relationships and fantasy transference relationships to the analyst.
>
> Naturally (indeed very often) the patient will turn to political or Political issues from time to time, but it is not the analyst's job to take these at face value or to discuss them in the ordinary sense with the patient. While my experience suggests some people (even analysts) can get confused on this point, and get caught up in being teachers or counsellors or advisers (or even sympathizers or opponents) in the consulting room I think it is absolutely clear that the principles of psychoanalytic treatment (as they were set out by Freud and subsequently developed by psychoanalysts) do not provide a basis for a psychoanalyst *qua* psychoanalyst to relate to his patient's material except as I set out above.

The point I would make here is that one cannot engage with the political in the consulting room without engaging with the politics of our profession itself.

These seven objections do need to be taken seriously and I think I have taken them seriously. I have tried to suggest where there is some mileage in them, and where I think a firm reply can be made.

## The therapeutic value of political discussion

Now I want to move on to the first of my positive proposals concerning the therapeutic value of political discussion in the session. Here, I will bring in the experiences of important practitioners in other fields who sought to politicize the practices of their own fields.

The German dramatist Bertolt Brecht conceived of the idea of a politicized theatre and developed a whole body of practices to go with that notion. Some of his practices, which constitute a sort of Brechtian clinical theory, are relevant to psychotherapy. For example, consider his well-known idea of the alienation effect, or 'distanciation effect'. Via certain technical theatrical devices, the audience is encouraged to step back and to distance itself from the drama going on on the stage in order to apperceive more clearly what the social, political and economic dynamics of the drama are. The intention is that the audience should not only *identify* emotionally with the characters in the play but should also try to *understand* and analyse what it is that those characters are doing. Brecht replaces involvement in theatre with what I would call *ex*volvement. In psychotherapy practice, it is possible to conceive of a therapeutic situation in which therapist and client get *ex*volved, without worrying that this could be a transgression of the principle that requires maximum emotional involvement and identification with the issues being processed in the therapy. Brechtian exvolvement serves, in very general terms, as a helpful model for the introduction of political discussion in the session as a therapeutic tool.

Another parallel is even more pertinent, and it concerns certain developments in feminist art practice, in particular what could be described as the framing of the everyday. For example, in 1976 the feminist conceptual artist Mary Kelly produced a work which became notorious, called *Post-Partum Document*. This was a record of her evolving relationship with her son over the first few years of his life. The part that everybody remembers, and on which I will concentrate, is the first room of *Post-Partum Document* in which the only works on show were the faeces- and urine-stained nappy (diaper) liners of this little boy, backed by white vellum, well framed and hung on the walls of the Hayward Gallery in London. The condition of the nappy liner showed how ill or healthy the baby (or his bowels) were at any one moment. Kelly could therefore track and comment upon her 'success' as a mother. The irony and political pointedness were deliberate.

A similar art work was created by Cate Elwes in 1979, called *Menstruation 2*. Seated on a clear perspex stool in a clear perspex booth in a white, diaphanous dress with no underwear or sanitary towels during the time of her period, she would allow the menstrual blood to flow, staining the garment, all the while dialoguing with an audience that surrounded this booth about what the wider implications of her female bodily processes were, what they meant to her, and about what the audience thought was going on.

Mentioning these art works is not intended to start a discussion about conceptual and feminist art. But these works worked because the ordinary was framed, whether in the traditional frame of a picture, in which the artist puts a stained nappy liner, or by the frame of the perspex booth in which a bleeding woman stains her garments before spectators and discusses it with them. My argument is that political discussion within the therapy frame will be different from ordinary political discussion in bar, living room or workplace. Just as menstruation, framed in the way I described, ceases to be menstruation and becomes conceptual art and has an impact in the cultural sphere, so, too, a discussion of politics in a therapy situation that, if transcribed, would look ordinary takes on a wholly other significance. Contained within the therapy vessel or frame (itself a therapy term), the ordinary becomes something other, and enters the psychological processes of therapist and client in a way that may be profoundly un-settling, possibly clarifying, and occasionally transformative. If we seek to explore the meaning and relevance of the political for ourselves and our clients, then an espousal of political discussion, in which the therapist has to make all the usual therapist decisions about his or her degree of involvement, openness and about the timing, is one way to proceed. Perhaps it is necessary to try it to see what happens. For a practitioner reading this who already discusses politics with clients, maybe these thoughts will help to theorize what is presently being done on an intuitive or ethical basis. There are simply no books or articles about the matter.

## The political myth of the person

The next proposal concerns what I call the political myth of the person. Is there such a thing as a person's political development? Just as we refer to psychological development generally, or people talk about how they have or have not developed over a lifetime, there might be a way of approaching politics on the personal level that can make use of the idea of development without getting hooked up on linear, normative and mechanistic notions of development.

How does the political person grow and develop? An individual person lives not only her or his life but also the life of the times. Jung told his students that 'when you treat the individual you treat the culture'. Persons cannot be seen in isolation from the society and culture that has played a part in forming them – as much feminist thinking has demonstrated.

Once we see that there is a political person who has developed over time, we can start to track the political history of that person – the way the political events of her or his lifetime have impacted on the forming of their personality. So we have to consider the politics a person has, so to speak, inherited from their family, class, ethnic, religious, national background – not forgetting the crucial questions of their sex and sexual orientation. Sometimes, people take on their parents' politics; equally often, people reject what their parents stood for. Social class often functions within the unconscious and sometimes I have found that it is the social class issues of the socially mobile client's parents that are truly significant.

But all this is a bit too rational. If there is something inherently political about humans – and most people think there is – then maybe the politics a person has cannot only be explained by social inheritance. Maybe there is an accidental, constitutional, fateful and inexplicable element to think about. Maybe people are just born with different amounts and kinds of political energy in them.

If that is so, then there would be implications both for individuals and for our approach to politics. What will happen if a person with a high level of political energy is born to parents with a low level of it (or vice versa)? What if the two parents have vastly different levels from each other? What is the fate of a person with a high level of political energy born into an age and a culture that does not value such a high level, preferring to reward lower levels of political energy? The answers to such questions shape not only a person's political myth but the shape and flavour of the political scene in their times.

The questions can get much more intimate. Did your parents foster or hinder the flowering of your political energy and your political potential? How did you develop the politics you have at this moment? In which direction are your politics moving, and why? I do not think these questions are presently on either a mainstream or an alternative political agenda. Nor are they on the agenda of many therapists or analysts.

My interest is not in what might be called political maturity. No such universal exists, as evaluations by different commentators of the same groups as 'terrorists' or 'freedom fighters' shows. My interest is in how people got to where they are politically and, above all, in how they themselves think, feel, explain and communicate about how they got to where they are politically – hence my reference to the political myth of the person. From a psychological angle, it often turns out that people are not actually where they thought they were politically, or that they got there by a route they did not know about.

In therapy, we can explore how the client got to where he or she is politically and, above all, how the clients themselves think, feel, explain and communicate about how they got to where they are politically; a subjective narrative of political development. We ask how a person *became* a Hampstead liberal, not whether being a Hampstead liberal is a good thing in itself – whilst not denying that we have a viewpoint about Hampstead liberals. Moreover, not all Hampstead liberals became Hampstead liberals in the same way. We want to know how Hampstead liberals have experienced their becoming Hampstead liberals.

When a client describes his or her political experiences, in the sense of formative or crucial political experiences, an analyst or therapist would listen with the same mix of literal and metaphorical understanding with which he or she would listen to any kind of clinical material – but with the ideas of political myth and political development in mind as permanent heuristic presences. Sometimes, the most productive path to follow would be to accept the client's account of his or her political history; at other times, what the client may have to say may be understood as image, symbol and metaphor; at other times, as defensive and/or distorted; sometimes, it will be a mélange of these ways of understanding; sometimes, a tension or competition may exist between them. In a sense, all of this moves us towards a conception of what could be called the 'psychological citizen'.

The implications for depth psychology of taking in these ideas about political development could be profound. In 1984 I suggested to my fellow members of the training committee of a psychotherapy organization that we should start to explore with candidates something about their political development – its history, roots, antecedents, patterns, vicissitudes and current situation – just as we looked into sexuality, aggression and spiritual or moral development. At that time, the idea was regarded as a bit way out but more recently it has evoked a favourable response. Similarly, if political and social factors are part of personality and psychological development, should not analysts and therapists explore those areas in initial interviews with prospective clients?

Incidentally, here, as so often, I have found that what looks like new theory is really only a necessary theorization of cutting-edge practice. In the survey, when I asked the respondents to say something about their own political histories and what had influenced their own political development, they tended to cover the same ground as I have covered in this section of the paper, though with very wide linguistic, conceptual and hermeneutic variations.

Why do I refer to political 'development'? Might this not be rather conservative from an intellectual standpoint? There are now numerous books on 'moral development', 'spiritual development', 'religious development'. And 'the development of personality' is a well-researched and much-argued-over field. So the general idea of development seems to be in the *Zeitgeist*. The idea of development is obviously intended to be applied as non-normatively, non-judgementally and non-positivistically as possible, though it will be as well for me to admit immediately that my own personal political beliefs and values will enter the picture and help to bring a kind of hierarchy into play. This is absolutely unavoidable, but I do not believe that my having beliefs and values of my own makes me any less neutral than or different from theorists in the fields of moral, spiritual, religious and personality development who undoubtedly have moral, spiritual, religious and psychological positions of their own to defend and privilege.

## The hidden politics of private, internal imagery

### The image of the parents in bed

My first proposal about the hidden politics of private, internal imagery concerns the primal scene – the image of father and mother together, the image of their intimate relationship, whether in bed or not. I have suggested on several occasions that primal-scene imagery functions as a kind of psychic fingerprint or trademark. Now I want to extend that idea in a political direction, to argue that the kind of image held of the parents' relationship to each other demonstrates, on the intrapsychic level, a person's capacity to sustain conflict constructively in the outer world – a crucial aspect of the person's political capacity. In the image of mother and father in one frame, the scene can be harmonious, disharmonious, one side may dominate the other side, one parent could be damaging the other parent, there will be patterns of exclusion, triumph, defeat, curiosity or total denial. These great and well-known primal-scene themes are markedly political. How they work out in the patient tells us something about that patient's involvement and investment in political culture and his or her capacity to survive therein.

I see the primal scene as a self-generated diagnostic monitoring of the person's psychopolitical state at any moment. The level of political development is encapsulated in the primal scene image. This is why images and assessments of the parental marriage change so much in the course of therapy or analysis. The parental marriage is not what changes in the majority of instances. Nor is it merely an increase in consciousness on the part of the patient which makes the image change. The image changes because the patient's inner and outer political styles and attitudes are changing. And the specificity of the image communicates what the new styles might be. The parents stand for a *process* as well as for particular attributes and capacities.

The experience of primal scene imagery may be additionally understood as an individual's attempt to function politically, coupling together into a unified whole his or her diverse psychic elements and agencies *without* losing their special tone and functioning. A sort of universalism versus multiculturalism on an individual level. What does the image of the copulating parents tell us about the political here-and-now of the client? The image of the parents in bed refers to an unconscious, pluralistic engagement by the client with all manner of sociopolitical phenomena and characteristics, many of which appear to him or her as so unlikely to belong together (to be bedfellows) that they are 'opposites', just as mother and father, female and male, passive and active sexual partners are said to be 'opposites', or 'whites' and 'blacks', or Israelis and Palestinians, or Catholics and Protestants, or rich and poor are regarded as irreconcilable political opposites.

Thus the question of the image of the parents in bed as a harmonious coming together of conflicting opposites can be worked on in more detail, according to the degree and quality of differentiation a person makes between the images of mother and father. For a primal scene only becomes fertile when the elements are distinguishable. In plain language, it's not a *stuck* image of parental togetherness that we see in a fertile primal scene, but something divided and unstuck, hence vital – but also linked, hence politically imaginable. The psyche (society) is trying to express its multifarious and variegated nature (multiculturalism) – and also its oneness and integration (universalism). Primal scene images can perform this pluralistic job perfectly and the message they carry concerns how well the job is going. Via primal scene imagery, the psyche is expressing the patient's pluralistic capacity to cope with the unity *and* the diversity of the political situation he or she is in. As Aristotle said, 'Similars do not a state make.'

I do not think that the reproductive heterosexuality of the primal scene should to be taken as excluding people of homosexual orientation. Far from it: I am convinced that the fruitfulness signified in the primal scene, and the problems therein, are completely congruent with homosexual experi-ence. I also think that there is a set of cultural and intellectual assumptions that need to be explicated. Why is it that psychological fecundity, variety and liveliness do not yet get theorized in homosexual terms? Why is psychological maturity still envisaged in a form of complementary wholeness that requires heterosexual imagery for it to work at all? Why do we not refer to a conjunction of *similars*? One could easily defend the thesis that heterosexual primal scene imagery works quite happily for persons of a homosexual orientation by recourse to metaphor, saying that primal scene heterosexuality refers not to the fact of reproduction but to the symbol of diversity, otherness, conflict, potential. Similarly, one could also point out that, since everyone is the result of a heterosexual union, hetero-sexual symbolism is simply inevitable and not excluding of a homosexual orientation. But I am dubious about these liberal manoeuvres because they still leave a question mark in my mind concerning the absence of texts replete with homosexual imagery that would perform the psychological and political functions of primal scene imagery. We might begin a search for the homosexual primal scene. Though this idea may sound controversial, it merely involves a recognition that the primal scene is about processes and functions and not about the actual parents. Hence the proposition that there could be a primal scene couched in gay or lesbian imagery will only cause problems to homophobic members of the psychotherapy world. We know by now how much psychoanalytic theory about homosexuality is little more than dressed-up prejudice, marching in step with the moral majority.

Personal narratives of primal scene imagery, and their working through, demonstrate to a considerable extent a person's capacity to sustain political conflict constructively. This general point about politics becomes more pertinent when applied to the professional politics of the field of depth psychology. Stuck parental imagery fits the field's symptoms of intolerance, fantasies of superiority, and difficulties with hearing the views of others. If depth psychology's primal scene imagery could be prodded into vigorous motion, perhaps by active ideological dialogue, I would feel more optimistic about its future.

The example I shall soon be giving of these ideas concerning political readings of primal scene imagery is the well-known general problem of not being able to imagine the parents' sexual life at all, or of having a bland and non-erotic image of it. Clearly, denial and repression play important parts in this, but my argument will be that to restrict our under-standing to these personal ego-defence mechanisms is to cut ourselves off from the plenitude of collective and public meanings in primal scene imagery.

Before discussing the 'non-primal scene', I want to say something further about why the primal scene is so important for politics. One particular reason for choosing to focus on the primal scene is that we are then invited to address the conventional twinning of man with active and woman with passive sexual behaviour. This twinning both reflects and, I think, inspires many gender divisions. When individuals access and work on their primal scene imagery, often in fantasy or via the transference in analysis, it is remarkable that the conventional male/active–female/passive divide does *not* invariably appear. Quite the reverse. In fact, it often seems as if the unconscious 'intention' of the sexual imagery associated with the primal scene is to challenge that particular definition of the differences between men and women. The challenge to the sexual status quo symbolizes a kind of secret challenge to the political status quo.

From the standpoint of gender politics, this discussion of the political relevance of a primal scene enables us to introduce the mother in a transmogrified and politicized form, as an active player in the sexual game and hence, potentially, as an active player in the political game.

Here, I am reminded of the Midrashic story of Lilith. She was, as readers will recall, the first consort of Adam, who was created from the earth at the same time as Adam. She was unwilling to give up her equality and argued with Adam over the position in which they should have intercourse, Lilith insisting on being on top. 'Why should I lie beneath you', she argued, 'when I am your equal, since both of us were created from dust?' But when Lilith saw that Adam was determined to be on top, she called out the magic name of God, rose into the air, and flew away. Eve was then created. Lilith's later career as an evil she-demon who comes secretly to men in the night (hence being responsible for nocturnal emissions) and as a murderer of newborns culminated, after the destruction of the temple, in a relationship with God as a sort of mistress. Lilith's stories are well documented by scholars of mythology. The importance for us is that the woman who demands equality with the man is forced to leave the Garden and gets stigmatized as the personification of evil.

What of the missing primal scene, the inability to imagine the parents' sexual life that I referred to earlier? I regard this non-primal scene as deriving in the first instance from a colossal fear of the consequences of conflict. (Again, sexual conflict symbolizing political conflict.) For, if the bodies of the parents are not in motion, then psychological and socio-political differences between them, including asymmetries and inequalities, need not enter consciousness. Over time, consciousness of political problematics impacts on the individual's internal processes, his or her capacity to experience different parts of the self in their own particularity and diversity whilst at the same time sensing that they participate in the whole in a more or less coherent sense of identity. The denied primal scene signifies a loss of faith in the political nature of the human organism and of society itself. Conversely, images of vigorous, mutually satisfying parental intercourse, including, perhaps, some kind of struggle for power, reveal a private engagement with the conflictual dynamics of the public sphere.

In my workshops, I get participants to do the following exercise. I ask them to divide a sheet of paper vertically. In the left-hand column, they are to list (1) their earliest memory (or fantasy of their earliest memory) of their parents' physical intimacy; (2) the same at adolescence; (3) the same today. In the right-hand column, they should list (1) their first political memory or the first time they became aware of political conflict; (2) their politics at adolescence and their general attitude to politics at that time; (3) the same today. The participants are asked to take home the piece of paper with its two columns – primal scene and politics. All they are asked to do is to reflect on what has been written down, scanning the entries in the two columns referring to each point in time and the developmental process revealed by a comparison of the two columns. The feedback has been fascinating; perhaps present readers would like to try the exercise.

## Dream imagery

An Italian client dreamt of a beautiful lake with clear deep water. He said this represented his soul and then immediately associated to the pollution on the Italian Adriatic coast. The image of the lake, and the association to coastal pollution, suggested, in the form of one symbol, the client's unconscious capacity for depth and his present state, of which he was all too conscious – a state of being clogged up by 'algae', like the coastal waters of the Adriatic. When disparate psychological themes are thrown together like this, the symbolic image makes a powerful impact on the individual, who cannot ignore it. In this particular instance, the notion that there was possibly a 'solution' for the clogging up of his lake/soul potential, and the idea that being clogged was a state he had gradually got into over time and was not a witch's curse, together with the vision that depth and clarity and beauty were options open to him, were powerful and liberating thoughts for the client to entertain. He made a choice to return to Italy, to tell his father that he was homosexual, and, in his words, to 'get more involved' – perhaps in environmental politics.

Returning to the dream of the lake, I would like to suggest an alternative reading, couched in more political terms. I think that this re-reading constitutes a further statement about the political properties of private, internal imagery. The images of the dream can be approached via their individual presence, or via their political presence, or via the movement and tension between the two. In the dream of the lake, the tension between the individual and the political presences of the image was prominent and insistent; after all, the client was Italian. What, the client and I asked together, is the role of pollution in the soul, or even in the world? What is the role of pollution in the achievement of psychological depth? Can the soul remain deep and clear while there is pollution in the world, in one's home waters? Did the lake, with intimations of mystery and isolation, clash with the popular, extroverted tourism of the Adriatic? Eventually, the patient's concern moved onto the social level: who owned the lake? Who should have access to such a scarce resource? Who would protect the lake from pollution? These were his associations. From wholly personal issues, such as the way his problems interfered with the flowering of his potential, we moved to political issues, such as the pollution of natural beauty, not only by industry but also by the mass extroversion of tourism. And we also moved back again from the political level to the personal level, including transference analysis. I do not mean to foreclose on other interpretations, but rather to add in a more 'political' one so that the client's unconsciously taken up political commitments can become clearer.

I think much imagery can be understood in therapy as performing this particular kind of transcendent or bridging function, transcending and bridging the gap between the apparently individual, private, subjective and the apparently collective, social, political. Much of this chapter argues for the general thesis that there is a constant relationship and articulation between the personal/subjective and the public/political dimensions of life. Can we discriminate these separate dimensions in such a way that eventually we can, on a more conscious level, better bring them together? I think we do find that private, internal imagery carries a public and political charge. Moreover, we need to be better placed to make practical, clinical use of the by-now conventional observation that the external world, particularly its social and power relations, has an effect on our subjective experience.

Applying this approach to imagery to a psychological analysis of the politics of the client, we would try to discriminate the individual and the social aspects of an image and see whether they can be brought to an equal level of consciousness. This process would increase the range of choices available to the client, rather than collapsing them into a solution. In the example, the question of ownership of the lake at first seemed a distant 'political' concern. But gradually the client's social sensitivity came to the fore: he asserted that the lake, like his soul, was not a commodity to be owned by anyone. Then a celebration of his social conscience came to the fore. He addressed the fate of his 'Italian-ness' on a personal, individual level. Finally, as the hidden politics of his imagery continued to pulse, he discovered more collective, cultural and political associations to pollution on the Adriatic. I hope it is clear that the public/political and private/subjective dimensions were both thoroughly alive.

This interpretive reworking of the imagery onto a sociopolitical level provides the beginnings of a model by which therapists and clients can track moves between individual and social realms and a means of studying conflicts and harmonies between culture and individual as these appear in the session. For individual and culture are not the crude opposites that many, including Freud, have taken them to be. Both terms enjoy the complex interaction produced by their dynamic relationship; the relationship changes the nature of the original 'opposites'. The more deep and personal the experience, the more political and public it may turn out to be.

The politics of imagery now operates, in the external world, at a pace that often precludes rational debate. If we are to avoid being permanently after-the-event – an unending social deferred action or *Nachträglichkeit* – then we have to try to engage with the political dimensions of psychological imagery.

## Citizen-as-therapist

My fourth proposal concerns ways in which the client, by modelling his or her thought processes and actions on those of the therapist, can find in the *method* of therapy itself a source of empowerment. Incidentally, the use of the word 'empowerment' does not preclude the recognition that its use may be disempowering. Whoever empowers has power; whoever is empowered lacks power. But this postmodern cliché has its own intellectual and moral limitations – in Hillel's words: 'If I am not for myself, who will be for me? If I am only for myself, what am I? And if not now, when?' Many clients (and therapists too) ask how we can translate our emotional, bodily and imaginative responses to Bosnia, to ecological disaster, to homelessness, to poverty worldwide, into action. How can someone begin to make political use of their private reactions to public events?

There is a sense in which this is the key political theme of our times: the ways in which we might translate passionately held political convictions – shall we call them political dreams? – into practical realities. I think it is possible to take a subjective approach to a political problem, maybe one that has been fashioned out of personal experience, and refashion that response into something that works – actually works – in the corridors of power. From a client's point of view, it is his or her political impotence and the consequent despair, hopelessness and self-disgust which may be addressed.

Virtually everyone reacts to either the political issues of the day or the political dimensions of experience in a private and often heartfelt way, but most of us diffidently assume that our cloistered responses are not really of much use in the objective world of 'real' politics. Even though we all know there *is* no objectivity when it comes to politics, we behave as if there were, in obedience to an ideology of civic virtue that cannot abide passion in the public sphere. For the powerful fear the dissident fantasies of the radical imagination.

Clinical therapy and analysis ponder the same kind of problem: how to translate the practitioner's private and subjective responses to the client (the 'counter-transference') into something that can, eventually, be fashioned into a useful intervention.

In their widely differing ways, therapists and analysts have, over time, managed to work out how do this – and this is my point. Therapists and analysts have already managed to privilege and valorize their subjectivity, seeing how its very construction within the therapy relationship gives it the potential to provide a basis for useful intervention in the session.

Therapists and analysts already have texts that teach them how to translate their impressions, intuitions, gut responses, bodily reactions, fantasies and dreams about clients into hard-nosed professional treatment approaches. They already have the idea that their subjective responses are precious, valid, relevant, effective – and there is some knowledge about how to do something with those responses.

So, without realizing it perhaps, we – therapists and clients – in the world of psychology and therapy *do* possibly have something that could be shared with the disempowered, with political activists – or made use of when we ourselves get politically active. For example, most clinicians know that their bodily reactions to the client's material are a highly important pathway to the client's psychic reality. Similarly, it is possible to honour and deploy the bodily reactions citizens have in response to the political world and the culture's social reality. After all, just as client and therapist are in it together, so, too, do citizen and political problem inhabit – quite literally – the same space.

All citizens – not just those involved in therapy – could start to function as therapists of the political world, learning to use their bodily and other subjective reactions as organs of political wisdom, helping them to understand the problems of the political more deeply and guiding the course of their actions. It would be another way to speak the political.

The evolution of a kind of political knowledge analogous to the therapeutic encounter would reflect the fact that so many people already possess a therapeutic attitude to the world. Many of us want to participate in nothing less than the resacralization of our culture by becoming therapists of the world. But it is hard to see how to go about it.

I certainly did not invent the notion that citizens have bodily and other subjective reactions to the political – we all know of that from our own experience of our own bodies and our own subjectivities in the political world. But it may be a novel contribution to suggest, as I do, that the political, with its problems, its pain, its one-sidedness, may actually be trying to communicate with us, its therapists. Does the political really want therapy? Will it come to its first session? Will the unconscious of the political and the several unconsciousness of us, its therapists, get into good-enough communication?

Here I am trying to do something with what is already known about citizens and the political – but not, as yet, much theorized over. I see this 'therapeutic' way of speaking and doing politics, not as something regrettable, an over-personal, hysterical approach to politics – rather, I see it as one path left open to us in our flattened, controlled, cruel and dying world. What official politics rejects as shadow – and what can undoubtedly still function as shadow – turns out to have value. Isn't that a typical pattern of discovery in therapy anyway?

Putting the citizen in the therapist's seat is itself a dramatic and radical move. For, in many psychoanalytic approaches to politics, the citizen is put firmly in the patient's seat, or on the couch: citizen as infant. Then the citizen has to be regarded as having only an infantile *transference* to politics. It is certainly not as empowering as having a counter-transference and it is the therapist's right to speak – the therapist's power – that I want clients to seize hold of and to spread around.

This strategy for empowerment is a further psychological extension of that fundamental feminist insight that the personal realm reflects the political realm, that what we experience in the subjective world can be the basis of progressive action and change in the political world.

I am trying to explore these ideas at public workshops as well as in therapy sessions. At a workshop in New York shortly after the Los Angeles riots of 1965, I asked a largely non-professional audience to imagine themselves as 'therapists' of a 'client' called 'the LA riots' and to record their physical, bodily and fantasy responses to their client (i.e. to track the 'counter-transference'). Unexpectedly, just doing the exercise itself created a cathartic effect. Participants eagerly reported how they had often reacted somatically or in other markedly subjective forms to political events. But they feared these responses would not pass muster in everyday political discourse. Their conception of politics was conditioned by the notions of 'objectivity' that I mentioned earlier; they had bought the con trick of the powerful.

When we came to discuss the riots in more rational vein, a whole range of novel, imaginative and practical ideas about urban and ethnic problems came out of the group process of this audience. Moreover, 'the political' was redefined, reframed, revisioned. Most of those present did not believe that there were avenues available in official political culture for what often gets stigmatized as an irrational approach. I think their assessment is right.

Utilizing a perspective derived from one hundred years of the practice of therapy, in which so-called irrational responses are honoured and heeded, is a small beginning in creating a new, more psychological approach to the problems of power and politics.

Lest it be thought that only an American audience could manage to do the exercise described just now, let me say that I have found similar reactions in Brazil, working with people in liberation theology, in Leningrad (as it then was) working with young Russian therapists hungry to marry their inner worlds with what was going on around them, and in Britain.

I feel that this kind of politics, this other way of speaking the political, favours participation by those who are presently on the margins of power: women, gay men and lesbians, members of ethnic minorities, those in transgressive families, the physically challenged, the economically disadvantaged, psychiatric patients. These are the people with whom therapists and clients should stand shoulder to shoulder – in the same ethos of unknowing and humility and respect for the wisdom of the other that characterizes all good clinical work.

For those diverse groupings should not be regarded as Marx's hopeless lumpenproletariat. Rather, they are the last untapped sources of new energies and ideas into the political and social realms. Disempowered people certainly do need the kind of economic and financial transfusions that only politics of the official kind can presently broker. But they also need validation from the profession that makes its living and derives its authority – its power – out of working with the feelings, fantasies, behaviours and embodiments that are banned and marginalized in life in the late modern world. There is a potential in everyone to be a therapist of the world. Throughout our lives, all of us have had private responses to politics. We need to raise to the level of cultural consciousness the kind of politics that people have carried within themselves secretly for so long. The therapy client, armed with therapy's own power to make something useful out of subjectivity, can take his or her place as citizen-as-therapist.

## A socialized, transpersonal psychology of community

In contemporary Western politics the buzz word is 'community'. Aside from the politicians, many clients also speak in therapy of a sense of pulling together that used to exist and is now lost. They feel the loss keenly. For other clients, the idea of community is more proactive, referring to a new kind of egalitarian politics based on their belief in what is shared, held in common, faced together. Communitarian thinking will (hopefully) both refresh our ideas of the state and, for many amongst this group of clients, of the power dynamics of the therapeutic relationship.

It is extraordinary that in the many lucid discussions about community that are taking place, there has been little space for a psychological contribution. Communitarian politics requires an overtly socialized psychology and when we try to create one we find that it will have, at some level, to be a transpersonal psychology. Politics is also a transpersonal activity and, like most transpersonal activities, politics points in what can only be described as a spiritual direction. Psychotherapy is not a religion, though it may be the heir to some aspects of conventional religion. The project of factoring the psychological into the political seems to want to be done in quasi-religious language. Perhaps this is because psychotherapy, politics and religion all share, at some level, in the fantasy of providing therapy for the world. The very word 'fantasy' must, I am sure, create problems for some readers. Fantasy is not in itself pathological and there is a necessarily utopic role for fantasy in political discourse.

Sometimes I see psychotherapy as a new monasticism, meaning that just as the monks and nuns kept culture in Europe alive during the so-called 'Dark Ages', so, too, in their often equally rigorous way, the therapists and analysts are keeping something alive in our own age. However, the values that psychotherapy keeps alive are difficult to classify. They do not always have the ring of absolute Truth (though such a possibility is not ruled out); nor are they based on a fixed account of human nature (though that is what is invariably being attempted, time and again). In its discovery of values and value in that which other disciplines might reject, psychotherapy helps to keep something alive in the face of threats ranging from state hegemony, to vicious market forces, to nostalgic longings for a return to a past in which it is assumed that the old certitudes of nation, gender and race would still hold.

We sometimes hear calls for a global ethic or a global sense of responsibility to be placed at the heart of political theory and the political process. My question is: how can this be done without some kind of psychological sensitivity and awareness? Such sensitivity and awareness may not be easily measurable by the sturdy tools of empiricism but reveal themselves in dream, in parental and primal-scene imagery, in an understanding of a person's own political history, development and myth. Hence, clinical work on oneself coexists with political work in one's society.

My working out of a 'clinical' model with which to engage political problematics is intended to make every citizen into a potential therapist of the world. An active role for the citizen-as-therapist is highlighted and nowhere will this be more apparent than in relation to experts (myself included). People's active, generative, inventive, compassionate potential is not being tapped and, as I see it, in order to tap into that kind of energy we need a reinvention of politics inside and outside the therapy session.

## Notes

1 I have tried to be careful in my use of the words 'politics' or 'the political', 'culture', 'society' and the 'collective'. By 'culture', I mean the assembly, limited in time and space, of the social, material, mental, spiritual, artistic, religious and ritual processes of a relatively stable and sizeable community. I use the words 'society' or 'societal' in the following senses: the means by which relations between individual and others are structured; the institutions that cause differences between individuals to acquire significances beyond those individual differences; whatever promotes learnt forms of behaviour and communication that excite support and approval or condemnation and punishment; relations between organizations and groups. The 'collective' implies what is held in common, ranging from a biological/phylogenetic use of collective to something like the collective atmosphere in a crowded theatre or soccer stadium.

2 I am aware that there are problems with the use of the term 'person'. I think that the need to retain some idea of the person is necessary when we consider the political dimensions of life. Paradoxically, my speculations about the political person and the political development of the person are part of, not in opposition to, attempts to decentre the habitual focus of psychoanalysis on an individual by evoking the place of the in-between, thus helping to dissolve the logic of inner and outer. Nor am I forgetting the wounded and grieving nature of the late modern or postmodern political person: that is why politics is a matter for therapists.

## References

Brown, Dennis and Zinkin, Louis (1994). *The Psyche and the World: Developments in Group-Analytic Theory*, London and New York: Routledge.

Gralnick, Alexander (1990). Review of Levine, Howard et al. (eds), *Psychoanalysis and the Nuclear Threat: Clinical and Theoretical Studies*. *International Journal of Mental Health* 20/1, pp. 67–69.

Hillman, James and Ventura, Michael (1992). *We've Had a Hundred Years of Psychotherapy and the World is Getting Worse*, San Francisco: Harper.

Levine, Howard et al. (eds) (1988). *Psychoanalysis and the Nuclear Threat: Clinical and Theoretical Studies*, Hillsdale, NJ: Analytic Press.

Samuels, Andrew (1993). *The Political Psyche*, London and New York: Routledge.

Samuels, Andrew (1994). 'Replies to an international questionnaire on political material brought into the clinical setting by clients of psychotherapists and analysts'. *International Review of Sociology* 3, pp. 7–60.

Samuels, Andrew (1998). 'Responsibility'. In *Development through Diversity: The Therapist's Use of Self*. London: United Kingdom Council for Psychotherapy.

# Index